East Bus Handbook

September 1993

British Bus Publishing

The North East Bus Handbook

The North East Bus Handbook is part of the Bus Handbook series that details the fleets of stage carriage and express coach operators. These are published by *British Bus Publishing* and cover Scotland, Wales and England north of London. Companion volumes, The North West Bus Handbook, The Yorkshire Bus Handbook and The Eastern Bus Handbook are currently available. Handbooks for East Midlands, Central and Wales are planned for 1994. Together with the London Bus Handbooks, South East Buses and South West Buses published by Capital Transport, they provide comprehensive coverage of all the principal operators' fleets in the British Isles.

Quality photographs for inclusion in these, and other areas covered by the series are welcome, though the publishers cannot accept responsibility for any loss. Details of changes to fleet information are also welcome.

More information on the Bus Handbook series is available from:

British Bus Publishing,
The Vyne,
16 St Margaret's Drive
Wellington
Telford,
Shropshire TF1 3PH

Series Editor: Bill Potter
Principal Editors for *The North East Bus Handbook:*
David Donati, David Little and Steve Warburton

Acknowledgements:
We are grateful to Keith Grimes, Ian Hope, Mark Jameson, John Jones, Colin Lloyd, Geoff Mills, Steve Sanderson, the PSV Circle and the operating companies for their assistance in the compilation of this book.

The front cover photo is by Steve Warburton
The rear cover and frontispiece photographs are by Michael Fowler, Bill Potter and Keith Grimes.

Contents correct to September 1993

ISBN 1 897990 03 0
Published by *British Bus Publishing*
The Vyne, 16 St Margarets Drive, Wellington,
Telford, Shropshire, TF1 3PH
© British Bus Publishing, September 1993

Contents

Overleaf, Top: Sunderland and District, part of the Go-Ahead Northern group, use the Wear Buses fleetname on an attractive green and grey livery. Leyland National 2, 4663 (UPT663V), is seen heading for Durham in early 1993. *Keith Grimes*

Overleaf, Bottom: The Leyland Lynx was the successor to the Leyland National on the Leyland/Volvo assembly line at Lillyhall, Cumbria. One of the earlier models of the Lynx is Busways 115 (F115HVK) now carrying the Economic livery used by one of the units based at South Shields. *Michael Fowler*

A LINE COACHES

A Line Coaches, Unit 1, Green Lane Industrial Estate, Pelaw, Gateshead,
Tyne & Wear, NE10 0OW

XRW519S	Bedford YMT	Plaxton Supreme III	C53F	1978	Ex Hall, Wallsend, 1980
CUI20	Van Hool T815	Van Hool Alicron	C49FT	1984	
C588ORG	Leyland Royal Tiger RT	Van Hool Alizée	C49FT	1986	
E695UND	Mercedes-Benz 609D	Made-to-Measure	B21F	1987	
H815LFS	Mercedes-Benz 814D	PMT Ami	C33F	1990	
H354GRY	Dennis Javelin 12SDA1919	Caetano Algarve	C53F	1991	

Livery: White and red

Previous Registrations:
CUI20   B383FNL

The only Dennis Javelin and sole example of the Caetano body in the A Line fleet is the status of H354GRY. It was photographed as it worked an excursion returning attendees from York Races to Tyneside. *David Little*

AMBERLINE

D Boyd, Earsdon Road, West Monkseaton, Whitley Bay, Tyne & Wear, NE25 9SX

C511DYM	Iveco Daily 49.10	Robin Hood City Nippy	B21F	1985	Ex London Buses, 1991
D580EWS	Freight Rover Sherpa 374	Dormobile	B16F	1986	Ex Badgerline, 1990
E629AMA	Iveco Daily 49.10	Carlyle Dailybus 2	B25F	1988	Ex Trent, 1993
G276TST	Leyland-DAF 400	Dormobile	B18F	1989	Ex Magicbus, Perth, 1990

Livery: Orange and red

Towards the end of 1992 Boyd, Whitley Bay adopted a red and orange livery together with the Amberline identity. A former London Buses Iveco Daily with Robin Hood bodywork, C511DYM, is seen during April 1993 loading passengers in Blackett Street, Newcastle.
Keith Grimes

The newest vehicle in the Amberline fleet is Dormobile-bodied Freight Rover Sherpa G276TST. New to Inverness Traction, it was photographed in May 1993 when leaving Whitley Bay bus station on service 342 to North Shields. *Keith Grimes*

ARMSTRONGS

Armstrong's Motor Service Ltd, Majestic Garage, Ebchester, Co Durham, DH8 0PQ

RUP565M	Leyland Leopard PSU3B/4R	Plaxton Derwent	B60F	1974	
WFH180S	Leyland Leopard PSU3E/4R	Plaxton Supreme III	C53F	1978	Ex NT West, 1983
JUP6T	Leyland Leopard PSU3E/3R	Plaxton Supreme III	C53F	1978	Ex Weardale, Stanhope, 1989
KRN109T	Leyland Leopard PSU3E/4R	Duple Dominant II Express	C47F	1978	Ex Cumberland, 1986
EYH802V	Volvo B58-61	Duple Dominant II Express	C50F	1980	Ex Buddens, Romsey, 1992
D855FRF	Volvo B10M-61	Plaxton Paramount 3500 III	C49FT	1987	Ex Happy Days, Woodseaves, 1992
E330MHN	Scania K112CRB	Plaxton Paramount 3500 III	C53FT	1988	
E340MHN	Scania K112CRB	Van Hool Alizée	C55FT	1988	
F265KTN	Mercedes-Benz 609D	Reeve Burgess Beaver	C25F	1988	
F266KTN	Mercedes-Benz 609D	Reeve Burgess Beaver	C25F	1988	
F821PBP	Mercedes-Benz 709D	Wadham Stringer	B25F	1989	Ex Rennie, Dunfermline, 1990
F999UEF	Scania K113CRB	Plaxton Paramount 3500 III	C50FT	1989	
F30UHN	Scania K113CRB	Plaxton Paramount 3500 III	C50FT	1989	
G23UJR	Scania K93CRB	Plaxton Derwent	B57F	1990	

Livery: Two tone blue or white

Previous Registrations:
D855FRF   D814SGB, WHA325

In recent years Armstrongs adopted a plain white livery in preference to their traditional two-tone blue. Later second-hand arrivals, however, have re-introduced the former livery. The newest vehicle in the current fleet is G23UJR, a Scania K93 with Plaxton Derwent bodywork, one of only nine such vehicles built. *David Little*

BARRIE PATTERSON TRAVELSURE

B Patterson, 72 King Street, Seahouses,
Northumberland, NE68 7XS

GMB878T	Bedford YMT	Plaxton Supreme III	C53F	1978	Ex Battrick & Brown, Blackburn, 1990
AHH35Y	Van Hool T815H	Van Hool Alicron	C49FT	1983	Ex Titterington, Blencowe, 1989
A322XHE	Leyland Royal Tiger B54	Plaxton Paramount 3500	C49F	1984	Ex Argyll, Greenock, 1992
B416DHK	Iveco 315-8-17	Berkhof Elk	C25F	1985	Ex R & I, London, 1992
C42JMA	Iveco 79.14	Caetano Viana	C25F	1986	Ex Barnes, Bedlington, 1988

Previous Registrations:
AHH35Y   LYS507Y, 212VPF

Livery: White and blue

Barrie Patterson Travelsure operates a service from Seahouses to Newcastle and the Metro Centre. Iveco 79F14, C42JMA, with Caetano bodywork is seen at Haymarket, Newcastle during May 1993. *Keith Grimes*

BEDLINGTON & DISTRICT

Bedlington & District Luxury Coaches Ltd, North Seaton Industrial Estate, Ashington
Northumberland, NE63 0YB

YVO270M	Bedford YRT	Duple Dominant Express	C53F	1973	Ex Barton, 1981
WHN582M	Bristol LH6L	Eastern Coach Works	B43F	1974	Ex Go-Ahead Northern, 1990
GUP912N	Bristol LH6L	Eastern Coach Works	B43F	1975	Ex Teesside, 1990
LTL663P	Bristol LH6L	Eastern Coach Works	B43F	1975	Ex Elfed High School, Buckley, 1990
SBR881P	Leyland Leopard PSU3C/4R	Plaxton Supreme III	C49F	1976	Ex Busways, 1989
PTT71R	Bristol LH6L	Plaxton Supreme III Express	C43F	1976	Ex United, 1991
WEX930S	Bristol LH6L	Eastern Coach Works	DP39F	1978	Ex Tyne & Wear Omnibus, 1990
YAW221T	Bedford YMT	Duple Dominant II Express	C53F	1978	Ex Owen, Oswestry, 1987
BNB236T	Leyland Leopard PSU5C/4R	Duple Dominant II	C50F	1979	Ex Brownrigg, Egremont, 1992
EBD233T	Leyland Leopard PSU3E/4RT	Plaxton Supreme III Express	C49F	1979	Ex Clarkes, Tredegar, 1993
EBD236T	Leyland Leopard PSU3E/4RT	Plaxton Supreme III Express	C49F	1979	Ex Clarkes, Tredegar, 1993
KBD21V	Bristol LHS6L	Eastern Coach Works	B30F	1979	Ex Robson, Thornaby, 1991
C394MHH	Ford Transit 190	Mellor	DP16F	1985	Ex Mason, Maryport, 1992
D164OWJ	Freight Rover Sherpa 350	Whittaker	M16	1986	Ex Hurst & Leak, Goose Green, 1992
D468YTN	Mercedes-Benz L608D	Reeve Burgess	DP19F	1988	Ex Busways, 1992
E812MVN	Ford Transit VE6	Dormobile	DP16F	1988	Ex Woodcock, Chadderton, 1992

Previous Registrations:

D468YTN	D839UCU, KSU462, D36YTN, 813VPU	SBR881P	JVK81P, 491JVX

Livery: White and blue

Bedlington and District's principle work over many years has been the transport of miners to the various collieries in Northumberland. In the past this has required double-deck buses, but today a mixture of Bristol, Bedford and Leyland coaches, and minibuses, are employed. KBD21V, a Bristol LHS with Eastern Coach Works bodywork is fitted with high-back seating, and was new to Northampton. *David Little*

J C BELL

J & R Bell, 1A Castlebeach Street, New Silksworth,
Sunderland, Tyne & Wear, SR3 1HJ

Depot: Strangford Road, Seaham.

WRE456L	Bedford YRT	Plaxton Elite III	C53F	1973	Ex Hill, Congleton, 1985
NBT369M	Leyland Leopard PSU3B/4R	Duple Dominant	C53F	1973	Ex Palmer, Carlisle, 1990
PJR157M	Volvo B58-56	Plaxton Elite III Express	C53F	1974	Ex Hunter, Seaton Delaval, 1992
GPA633V	Volvo B58-61	Duple Dominant II	C57F	1980	Ex Thamesmead, SE18, 1983
KUB554V	Leyland Leopard PSU3E/4R	Plaxton Supreme IV Express	C49F	1980	Ex Dodsworth, Boroughbridge, 1991
RCD982X	MAN MT8.136	Reeve Burgess Riviera	C16DL	1982	Ex Skill, Nottingham, 1989
RML109Y	Volvo B10M-61	Plaxton Viewmaster IV	C49FT	1982	Ex Pettigrew, Mauchline, 1988
D853LND	Renault-Dodge S56	Northern Counties	B18F	1986	Ex GM Buses, 1992
D863LND	Renault-Dodge S56	Northern Counties	B18F	1986	Ex GM Buses, 1992
E521DCU	Mercedes-Benz L207D	Devon Conversions	M9L	1987	Ex Tyne & Wear Dial-A-Ride, 1989
E523DCU	Mercedes-Benz L307D	Devon Conversions	M9L	1987	Ex Tyne & Wear Dial-A-Ride, 1989
E524DCU	Mercedes-Benz L307D	Devon Conversions	M9L	1987	Ex Tyne & Wear Dial-A-Ride, 1989
H248MRD	Renault Master T35D	Atlas	M11	1991	
H249MRD	Renault Master T35D	Atlas	M11	1991	
J290SMO	Renault Master T35D	Atlas	M11	1991	
J291SMO	Renault Master T35D	Atlas	M11	1991	
J292SMO	Renault Master T35D	Atlas	M11	1991	
J294SMO	Renault Master T35D	Atlas	M11	1991	
J295SMO	Renault Master T35D	Atlas	M11	1991	
J296SMO	Renault Master T35D	Atlas	M11	1991	

Livery: Cream, blue and orange; or orange and yellow.

New to West Yorkshire Road Car, Leyland Leopard KUB554V has a Plaxton Supreme Express body and is seen near Sunderland city centre working service 45 from Seaham. A West Yorkshire destination blind from Leeds depot is still fitted unfortunately, because Sunderland has been able to claim city status since April 1992. *Phillip Stephenson*

BOB SMITH TRAVEL

Bob Smith Travel Ltd, Kingsway Garage, Esh Road, Langley Park, Co Durham.

PTE199S	AEC Reliance 6MUELS	Duple Dominant II(1977)	C53F	1962	Ex Smith, Wigan, 1979
KCN916J	Leyland Leopard PSU3B/4RT	Plaxton Elite II	C51F	1971	Ex Eagre, Morton, 1989
TUB20M	Leyland Leopard PSU3B/4RT	Plaxton Elite III	C51F	1974	Ex Citylink, 1993
MWW564P	Leyland Leopard PSU3C/4R	Plaxton Supreme III Express	C49F	1976	Ex On Target Training, 1993
OEW274R	Leyland Leopard PSU3C/4R	Plaxton Supreme III Express	C53F	1976	Ex Grasby, Oxhill, 1989
WGW579S	Leyland Leopard PSU5B/4R	Plaxton Supreme III	C53F	1978	Ex Dodsworth, Boroughbridge, 1992
VCD291S	Leyland Leopard PSU3E/4R	Duple Dominant II	C49F	1978	Ex Rennie, Dunfermline, 1990
EBM438T	Leyland Leopard PSU5C/4R	Duple Dominant II	C57F	1979	Ex Heslop, London, 1993
FRX869T	Leyland Leopard PSU5C/4R	Plaxton Supreme III	C53F	1978	Ex Rennie, Dunfermline, 1990
NLD7V	Leyland Leopard PSU5C/4R	Duple Dominant II	C57F	1979	Ex Yorkshire Rider, 1990
BVP796V	Leyland Leopard PSU3E/4R	Willowbrook Warrior(1990)	B47F	1980	Ex SUT, 1990
NAO807W	Mercedes-Benz L307D	Reeve Burgess	M12	1981	Ex Masters & Milburn, Craghead, 1982
LCU434X	Leyland Leopard PSU5C/4R	Duple Dominant IV	C57F	1981	
AOD650Y	Leyland Tiger TRCTL11/2R	Plaxton Supreme V	C57F	1983	Ex Dodsworth, Boroughbridge, 1992
YPY528Y	Mercedes-Benz L307D	Devon Conversions	C12F	1983	
B997JTN	Leyland Tiger TRCTL11/3R	Duple Laser	C57F	1985	
C463BHY	Ford Transit 190	Dormobile	B16F	1986	Ex City Line, 1993
D391SGS	Freight Rover Sherpa 374	Dormobile	B16F	1987	Ex Albany Coaches, Glasgow, 1990
D396SGS	Freight Rover Sherpa 374	Dormobile	B16F	1987	Ex Redwatch, East Calder, 1990
D424SKY	Scania K112CRB	Van Hool Alizée	C53F	1987	
E903DRG	Ford R1114	Plaxton Elite III	C53F	1988	
G148SUS	Mercedes-Benz 609D	Scott	C24F	1990	

Livery: White and blue

Previous Registrations:

FRX869T	YYJ302T, 406DCD	PTE199S	63DBU
KCN916J	GYK474J, 411HAT		

Named vehicles: D424SKY *Lady Sarah*, E903DRG *Lady Gail*.

BVP796V is unusual amongst Willowbrook Warrior-bodied Leyland Leopards in retaining its original registration. Now with Bob Smith Travel it is about to enter North Road, Durham on service 754 from its home village of Langley Park.
G R Mills

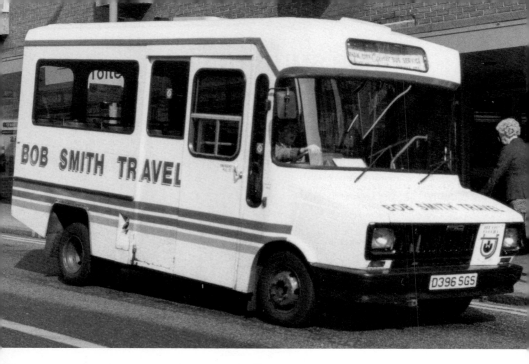

Durham City tourist attractions are served by a special route - the Durham City Courier bus service. Bob Smith Travel operates this facility and two of the vehicles employed are (above) a former Luton & District Sherpa, D396SGS and (below) a Mercedes-Benz 609D with Scott conversion, G148 SUS *Phillip Stephenson/Keith Grimes*

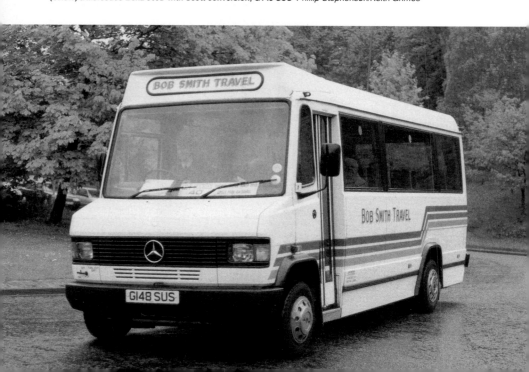

BOND BROS

Bond Bros Coaches, 75 High Street, Willington, Co Durham, DL15 0PF

PRH247G	Leyland Atlantean PDR1A/1	Roe	H44/31F	1969	Ex Kingston-upon-Hull, 1990
PRH248G	Leyland Atlantean PDR1A/1	Roe	H44/31F	1969	Ex Kingston-upon-Hull, 1990
UHG720R	Leyland National 11351A/1R		B49F	1978	Ex Ribble, 1993
UHG727R	Leyland National 11351A/1R		B49F	1978	Ex Ribble, 1993
DTL547T	Bristol LH6L	Eastern Coach Works	B43F	1978	Ex RoadCar, 1989
DKY867V	AEC Reliance 6U3ZR	Plaxton Supreme IV	C53F	1979	Ex Mosley, Barugh Green, 1983
XUP827V	Volvo B58-61	Plaxton Supreme IV	C50F	1980	Ex Prestige, Whitley Bay, 1990
BGR630W	Bedford YLQ	Duple Dominant II	C45F	1980	Ex Gypsy Queen, Langley Park, 1984
VLA40X	Bedford YMQ	Plaxton Supreme IV	C45F	1981	Ex C&M Cars, Laindon, 1990
C158UHN	MCW Metroliner DR130/10	MCW	CH55/17CT	1985	Ex Durham Travel, Hetton, 1992
E66SUH	Volkswagon LT55	Optare City Pacer	B25F	1988	Ex Bebb, Llantwit Fardre, 1990
H170EJU	Mercedes-Benz 814D	Reeve Burgess Beaver	C33F	1990	

Livery: Pale blue and cream

Previous Registrations:

VLA40X	VLA41X	XUP827V	OBD71V, 675BKH

For some years the destination of many Bristol LHs in the north east of England would have been the Trimdon group. Following the demise of TMS as an independant the number of such arrivals in the area has been limited. One of the few examples has been Bond Bros DTL547T, once a Lincolnshire Road Car vehicle. It is seen at Bishop Auckland bus station. *G R Mills*

The oldest vehicles currently owned are two Roe-bodied Leyland Atlanteans originating with Kingston-upon-Hull Corporation. These, the first double deckers in the Bond Bros fleet, were initially purchased for school contracts. Following the loss of school work the pair saw increased use on Bond Bros services. PRH248G was at Bishop Auckland bus station during May 1993 on their long-established Willington service. *Keith Grimes*

Bond Bros added two Leyland Nationals to their fleet at the beginning of 1993. One of the pair which were new to Ribble, UHG720R, is seen arriving at Bishop Auckland bus station during the following June. *J Carter*

The North East Bus Handbook

BUSWAYS

Busways Travel Services Ltd, Cuthbert House, Manors,
Newcastle-upon-Tyne, NE1 2EL

Depots: Shields Road, Byker (Armstrong Galley, Blue Bus, Newcastle Busways); Stamfordham Road, Slatyford (Newcastle Busways); Wheatsheaf, Sunderland (Sunderland Busways, Tyne & Wear Omnibus); Dean Road, Chichester, South Shields (Economic, South Shields); Hetton Lyons Industrial Estate, Easington Lane (Favourite).

3	ONL645X	Leyland Leopard PSU5D/4R	Plaxton Supreme V	C53F	1981	Ex Jumbulance project, 1986
4	KSU454	Leyland Tiger TRCTL11/3R	Van Hool Alizée	C50FT	1985	
5	KSU455	Leyland Tiger TRCTL11/3R	Van Hool Alizée	C50FT	1985	
6	KSU456	Leyland Tiger TRCTL11/3R	Van Hool Alizée	C53F	1985	
7	KSU457	Leyland Tiger TRCTL11/3RZ	Plaxton Paramount 3500 III	C53F	1988	
8	KSU458	Leyland Royal Tiger B54	Van Hool Alizée	C49FT	1986	
9	KSU459	Leyland Tiger TRCTL11/3RH	Van Hool Alizée	C48FT	1986	
14	644HKX	Leyland Tiger TRCTL11/3R	Plaxton Paramount 3500 III	C53F	1985	Ex Fowler, Holbeach, 1989
15	1JVK	Leyland Tiger TRCTL11/3RH	Plaxton Paramount 3500 III	C53F	1987	
16	2JVK	Leyland Tiger TRCL10/3ARZM	Plaxton Paramount 3200 III	C53F	1987	Ex Shearings, 1993
17	491JVX	Leyland Tiger TRCL10/3ARZM	Plaxton Paramount 3200 III	C53F	1987	Ex Shearings, 1993
18	552UTE	Leyland Tiger TRCL10/3ARZM	Plaxton Paramount 3200 III	C53F	1987	Ex Shearings, 1993
31	813VPU	Scania K113TRB	Van Hool Astrobel	CH53/14CT	1990	
32	KSU460	Scania K113TRB	Van Hool Astrobel	CH53/14CT	1990	
33	KSU463	Scania K113TRB	Van Hool Astrobel	CH53/14CT	1990	
34	KSU464	Scania K113TRB	Van Hool Astrobel	CH53/14CT	1990	
51	KSU461	MCW Metroliner DR130/5	MCW	CH53/16CT	1984	
55	KSU465	MCW Metroliner DR130/28	MCW	CH53/16DT	1986	
56	KSU466	MCW Metroliner DR130/29	MCW	CH53/17DT	1986	Ex London Buses, 1987
61	HTY139W	Leyland Leopard PSU3E/4R	Duple Dominant II Express	C49F	1980	Ex Grey-Green, London, 1988
62	HTY137W	Leyland Leopard PSU3E/4R	Duple Dominant II Express	C49F	1980	Ex Grey-Green, London, 1988
63	HTY138W	Leyland Leopard PSU3E/4R	Duple Dominant II Express	C49F	1980	Ex Grey-Green, London, 1988
65	TBC1X	Leyland Leopard PSU3F/4R	Plaxton Supreme IV Express	C53F	1981	Ex Nottingham, 1988
66	TBC2X	Leyland Leopard PSU3F/4R	Plaxton Supreme IV Express	C53F	1981	Ex Nottingham, 1988
71	CMJ447T	Leyland Leopard PSU3E/4R	Plaxton Supreme III	C53F	1979	Ex Southend, 1988

The coaching division of Busways Travel operates as Armstrong Galley using a blue livery with three bands of red, orange and yellow. Nearly all of these coaches now carry private registrations such as 4 (KSU454), a Leyland Tiger with the Van Hool Alizée style of body. Originally B104DVK, it was photographed at Gallowgate, Newcastle. *Keith Grimes*

The North East Bus Handbook

To replace some of the MCW Metroliners used on the Armstrong Galley Clipper service, four Scania K113TRB with Van Hool Astrobel double-deck bodies were purchased. No.31 (813VPU) was originally registered G31WTY and is seen during 1992 at Byker depot, Newcastle. However, since then the Clipper service has been withdrawn and the four Scanias have been painted into National Express Rapide livery for use on their services. *G R Mills*

Having served two Midlands municipalities, Leicester and Nottingham, two Leyland Leopards with Plaxton Supreme Express bodywork joined the Busways fleet in 1988. The second of the pair, 66 (TBC2X), was at Newcastle Haymarket in May 1993 wearing the Blue Bus Services livery. *Keith Grimes*

Opposite, Top: Central Newcastle provides the background to Newcastle Busways 424 (H424BNL). Based on the Scania N113DRB chassis is the Alexander RH-type body and it is one of ten such vehicles placed in service during 1991. One of its notable features is the electronic destination display. *Michael Fowler*

Opposite, Bottom: The types of vehicle most associated with the Busways fleet are the Alexander-bodied Leyland Atlanteans and Fleetlines produced in the late 1970s. Sunderland Busways 805 (OCU805R) is one based on a Leyland Fleetline chassis and shows the position of the near-side staircase. *Keith Grimes*

The North East Bus Handbook

101-125

		Leyland Lynx LX112L10ZR1S		Leyland		B49F	1988-89			
101	F101HVK	**106**	F106HVK	**111**	F111HVK	**116**	F116HVK	**121**	F121HVK
102	F102HVK	**107**	F107HVK	**112**	F112HVK	**117**	F117HVK	**122**	F122HVK
103	F103HVK	**108**	F108HVK	**113**	F113HVK	**118**	F118HVK	**123**	F123HVK
104	F104HVK	**109**	F109HVK	**114**	F114HVK	**119**	F119HVK	**124**	F124HVK
105	F105HVK	**110**	F110HVK	**115**	F115HVK	**120**	F120HVK	**125**	F125HVK

126	H126ACU	Leyland Lynx LX2R11C15Z4S	Leyland	DP47F	1990	
127	H127ACU	Leyland Lynx LX2R11C15Z4S	Leyland	DP47F	1990	

Preserved Fleet - The fleet numbers carried are in brackets, all registrations have been allocated from new.

B137	RCU499S	Metro-Scania BR111DH	MCW	H48/37F	1977	(499)
B140	LCU112	Daimler CCG6	Roe	H35/28R	1964	(140)
B141	WBR248	Atkinson Alpha PM746HL	Marshall	B45D	1964	(48)
B142	FBR53D	Leyland Panther PSUR1A/1R	Strachans	B47D	1966	(53)
B143	LVK123	Leyland Titan PD2/3	Leyland	H30/26R	1948	(123)

Busways operate a total of 27 Leyland Lynx shared between Sunderland Busways, South Shields Busways and Economic. One of the Sunderland Busways examples, 103 (F103HVK), is shown at the junction of Ryhope Road and Durham Road during March 1993. *Phillip Stephenson*

204-223

Leyland Atlantean AN68A/2R   Alexander AL   H49/37F   1980

204	EJR104W	208	EJR108W	212	EJR112W	217	EJR117W	221	EJR121W
205	EJR105W	209	EJR109W	213	EJR113W	218	EJR118W	222	EJR122W
206	EJR106W	210	EJR110W	214	EJR114W	219	EJR119W	223	EJR123W
207	EJR107W	211	EJR111W	215	EJR115W				

244-312

Leyland Atlantean AN68A/2R   Alexander AL   H49/37F   1978

244	SCN244S	258	SCN258S	270	SCN270S	283	SCN283S	297	UVK297T
247	SCN247S	259	SCN259S	271	SCN271S	284	SCN284S	298	UVK298T
248	SCN248S	260	SCN260S	273	SCN273S	285	SCN285S	299	UVK299T
249	SCN249S	261	SCN261S	274	SCN274S	286	SCN286S	300	UVK300T
250	SCN250S	262	SCN262S	275	SCN275S	287	UVK287T	301	VCU301T
251	SCN251S	263	SCN263S	276	SCN276S	288	UVK288T	302	VCU302T
252	SCN252S	264	SCN264S	277	SCN277S	289	UVK289T	303	VCU303T
253	SCN253S	265	SCN265S	278	SCN278S	290	UVK290T	304	VCU304T
254	SCN254S	266	SCN266S	279	SCN279S	291	UVK291T	309	VCU309T
255	SCN255S	267	SCN267S	280	SCN280S	292	UVK292T	310	VCU310T
256	SCN256S	268	SCN268S	281	SCN281S	294	UVK294T	312	VCU312T
257	SCN257S	269	SCN269S	282	SCN282S	295	UVK295T		

314-363

Leyland Atlantean AN68A/2R   Alexander AL   H49/37F   1980

314	AVK134V	324	AVK144V	334	AVK154V	344	AVK164V	354	AVK174V
315	AVK135V	325	AVK145V	335	AVK155V	345	AVK165V	355	AVK175V
316	AVK136V	326	AVK146V	336	AVK156V	346	AVK166V	356	AVK176V
317	AVK137V	327	AVK147V	337	AVK157V	347	AVK167V	357	AVK177V
318	AVK138V	328	AVK148V	338	AVK158V	348	AVK168V	358	AVK178V
319	AVK139V	329	AVK149V	339	AVK159V	349	AVK169V	359	AVK179V
320	AVK140V	330	AVK150V	340	AVK160V	350	AVK170V	360	AVK180V
321	AVK141V	331	AVK151V	341	AVK161V	351	AVK171V	361	AVK181V
322	AVK142V	332	AVK152V	342	AVK162V	352	AVK172V	362	AVK182V
323	AVK143V	333	AVK153V	343	AVK163V	353	AVK173V	363	AVK183V

Busways still operate a large number of the long-wheelbase Leyland Atlanteans, all with Alexander bodywork and delivered between 1976 and 1980. Kepple Street, South Shields is the setting for 299 (UVK299T) operating service X20 to Fellgate Estate, Jarrow. *Bill Potter*

368-405

				Leyland Fleetline FE30AGR		MCW			H43/32F		1979		
368	VCU368T	378	VCU378T	385	VCU385T	392	VCU392T	399	VCU399T
369	VCU369T	379	VCU379T	386	VCU386T	393	VCU393T	400	VCU400T
370	VCU370T	380	VCU380T	387	VCU387T	394	VCU394T	401	VCU401T
371	VCU371T	381	VCU381T	388	VCU388T	395	VCU395T	402	VCU402T
374	VCU374T	382	VCU382T	389	VCU389T	396	VCU396T	403	VCU403T
375	VCU375T	383	VCU383T	390	VCU390T	397	VCU397T	404	VCU404T
376	VCU376T	384	VCU384T	391	VCU391T	398	VCU398T	405	VCU405T
377	VCU377T								

413	JFT413X	Scania BR112DH	Alexander RH	H47/31F	1982
414	JFT414X	Scania BR112DH	Alexander RH	H47/31F	1982

421-430

				Scania N113DRB		Alexander RH			H47/29F		1990		
421	H421BNL	423	H423BNL	425	H425BNL	427	H427BNL	429	H429BNL
422	H422BNL	424	H424BNL	426	H426BNL	428	H428BNL	430	H430BNL

Opposite, Top: **Typical of Busways operation in South Shields is 368 (VCU368T). Built in 1979 it is a Leyland Fleetline FE30AGR with MCW bodywork.** *Michael Fowler*

Opposite, Bottom: **Blue Bus Services livery is carried by Busways 1701, the first of a pair of Dennis Darts with Reeve Burgess Pointer bodywork. Built in 1991, the production of the Pointer has since been transferred to the Plaxton works in Scarborough.** *Keith Grimes*

Below: **With a large fleet of MCW Metropolitans already owned it was with no surprise that Tyne and Wear PTE ordered two Scania BR112DH for evaluation. Fitted with Alexander RH-type bodies they now operate for Tyne and Wear PTE's successor, Busways. No.413 (JFT413X) is seen between duties outside the Central station in Newcastle.** *Bill Potter*

The North East Bus Handbook

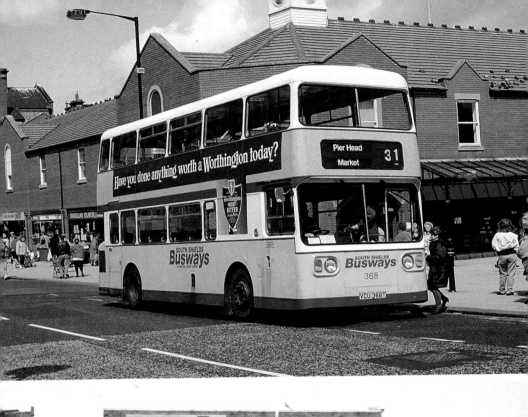

500-565

Leyland Atlantean AN68A/2R Alexander AL H48/33F* 1976 *540-4 are H48/34F

500	MVK500R	521	MVK521R	542	MVK542R	554	MVK554R	561	MVK561R
507	MVK507R	532	MVK532R	543	MVK543R	555	MVK555R	563	MVK563R
509	MVK509R	540	MVK540R	544	MVK544R	556	MVK556R	564	MVK564R
519	MVK519R	541	MVK541R	551	MVK551R	558	MVK558R	565	MVK565R

601-665

Leyland Olympian ONLXB/1R Alexander RH H45/31F 1985-86

601	C601LFT	615	C615LFT	628	C628LFT	641	C641LFT	654	C654LFT
602	C602LFT	616	C616LFT	629	C629LFT	642	C642LFT	655	C655LFT
603	C603LFT	617	C617LFT	630	C630LFT	643	C643LFT	656	C656LFT
604	C604LFT	618	C618LFT	631	C631LFT	644	C644LFT	657	C657LFT
605	C605LFT	619	C619LFT	632	C632LFT	645	C645LFT	658	C658LFT
606	C606LFT	620	C620LFT	633	C633LFT	646	C646LFT	659	C659LFT
608	C608LFT	621	C621LFT	634	C634LFT	647	C647LFT	660	C660LFT
609	C609LFT	622	C622LFT	635	C635LFT	648	C648LFT	661	C661LFT
610	C610LFT	623	C623LFT	636	C636LFT	649	C649LFT	662	C662LFT
611	C611LFT	624	C624LFT	637	C637LFT	650	C650LFT	663	C663LFT
612	C612LFT	625	C625LFT	638	C638LFT	651	C651LFT	664	C664LFT
613	C613LFT	626	C626LFT	639	C639LFT	652	C652LFT	665	C665LFT
614	C614LFT	627	C627LFT	640	C640LFT	653	C653LFT		

667-676

Leyland Olympian ON2R50C13Z4 Northern Counties Palatine H47/30F 1990

667	H667BNL	669	H669BNL	671	H671BNL	673	H673BNL	675	H675BNL
668	H668BNL	670	H670BNL	672	H672BNL	674	H674BNL	676	H676BNL

677-697

Leyland Olympian ONLXB/1RH Northern Counties H43/30F 1988 Ex London Buses, 1991

677	E901KYR	682	E909KYR	686	E914KYR	690	E919KYR	694	E923KYR
678	E905KYR	683	E910KYR	687	E915KYR	691	E920KYR	695	E924KYR
679	E906KYR	684	E911KYR	688	E917KYR	692	E921KYR	696	E925KYR
680	E907KYR	685	E912KYR	689	E918KYR	693	E922KYR	697	E927KYR
681	E908KYR								

When Bexleybus lost London Regional Transport services in the Bexleyheath area to other operators, a batch of Northern Counties bodied Leyland Olympians was redundant. Busways took delivery of 21 to update their fleet profile and 691 (E920KYR) at Four Lane Ends Metro station, is an example. *Keith Grimes*

The last batch of Leyland Olympians delivered to Busways had bodies by Northern Counties. Most of these are operated by the Sunderland Busways division and 667 (H667BNL) was photographed leaving Sunderland city centre on service 15 to Hastings Hill. Dot-matrix destination and route number equipment is fitted. *Steve Warburton*

Following the two Scania BR112DH in 1982 it was not until 1986 that further new double deckers for the Tyne and Wear PTE entered service, although the first arrived in December 1985. These vehicles were Leyland Olympians with Alexander R-type bodywork. One of the type is 624 (C624LFT), seen on New Bridge Street in Newcastle while operating one of the frequent routes to Killingworth. *Bill Potter*

800-839

| | | | | | | | | | Leyland Fleetline FE30AGR | Alexander AL | H44/30F | 1977 |

#	Reg	#	Reg	#	Reg	#	Reg	#	Reg
800	OCU800R	808	OCU808R	816	OCU816R	824	OCU824R	832	RCU832S
801	OCU801R	809	OCU809R	817	OCU817R	825	OCU825R	833	RCU833S
802	OCU802R	810	OCU810R	818	OCU818R	826	RCU826S	834	RCU834S
803	OCU803R	811	OCU811R	819	OCU819R	827	RCU827S	835	RCU835S
804	OCU804R	812	OCU812R	820	OCU820R	828	RCU828S	836	RCU836S
805	OCU805R	813	OCU813R	821	OCU821R	829	RCU829S	837	RCU837S
806	OCU806R	814	OCU814R	822	OCU822R	830	RCU830S	838	RCU838S
807	OCU807R	815	OCU815R	823	OCU823R	831	RCU831S	839	RCU839S

901-920

Scania N113CRB Alexander PS B51F 1988-89

#	Reg	#	Reg	#	Reg	#	Reg	#	Reg
901	F901JRG	905	F905JRG	909	F909JRG	913	F913JRG	917	F917JRG
902	F902JRG	906	F906JRG	910	F910JRG	914	F914JRG	918	F918JRG
903	F903JRG	907	F907JRG	911	F911JRG	915	F915JRG	919	F919JRG
904	F904JRG	908	F908JRG	912	F912JRG	916	F916JRG	920	F920JRG

921-926

Scania N113CRB Alexander PS B51F 1989-90

#	Reg	#	Reg	#	Reg	#	Reg	#	Reg
921	G921TCU	923	G923TCU	924	G924TCU	925	G925TCU	926	G926TCU
922	G922TCU								

| 927 | G113SKX | Scania N113CRB | Alexander PS | B51F | 1989 | Ex Scania demonstrator, 1991 |

928-937

Scania N113CRB Alexander PS B51F 1991

#	Reg	#	Reg	#	Reg	#	Reg	#	Reg
928	H428EFT	930	H430EFT	932	H432EFT	934	H434EFT	936	H436EFT
929	H429EFT	931	H431EFT	933	H433EFT	935	H435EFT	937	H437EFT

| 938 | G108CEH | Scania N113CRB | Alexander PS | B51F | 1990 | Ex Stevensons, 1993 |

A further batch of ten Scania N113CRB, again with Alexander PS-type bodywork, were added to the Busways fleet during 1991. The first of this batch, 928 (H428EFT), is seen in Market Street, Newcastle on service 1B to Longbenton. With the acquisition of second-hand examples, Busways has now accumulated 60 per cent of this type of vehicle in Britain. *Bill Potter*

1218	KBB118D	Leyland Atlantean PDR1/1R	MCW		O44/34F	1966		
1227	SVK627G	Leyland Atlantean PDR1A/1R	Alexander J		O44/30F	1969		

1401-1460

		Mercedes-Benz 709D		Reeve Burgess Beaver	B20F*	1986-87	*1431/49/51/3 are B23F	
							*1444 is DP23F	

1401	D401TFT	1413	D413TFT	1425	E425AFT	1437	E437AFT	1449	E449AFT
1402	D402TFT	1414	D414TFT	1426	E426AFT	1438	E438AFT	1450	E450AFT
1403	D403TFT	1415	D415TFT	1427	E427AFT	1439	E439AFT	1451	E451AFT
1404	D404TFT	1416	D416TFT	1428	E428AFT	1440	E440AFT	1452	E452AFT
1405	D405TFT	1417	D417TFT	1429	E429AFT	1441	E441AFT	1453	E453AFT
1406	D406TFT	1418	D418TFT	1430	E430AFT	1442	E442AFT	1454	E454AFT
1407	D407TFT	1419	D419TFT	1431	E431AFT	1443	E443AFT	1455	E455AFT
1408	D408TFT	1420	D420TFT	1432	E432AFT	1444	E444AFT	1456	E456AFT
1409	D409TFT	1421	E421AFT	1433	E433AFT	1445	E445AFT	1457	E457AFT
1410	D410TFT	1422	E422AFT	1434	E434AFT	1446	E446AFT	1458	E458AFT
1411	D411TFT	1423	E423AFT	1435	E435AFT	1447	E447AFT	1459	E459AFT
1412	D412TFT	1424	E424AFT	1436	E436AFT	1448	E448AFT	1460	E460AFT

1604	TPJ55S	Bristol LHS6L		Eastern Coach Works	B35F	1977	Ex South Yorkshire, 1986
1605	TPJ60S	Bristol LHS6L		Eastern Coach Works	B35F	1977	Ex South Yorkshire, 1986
1606	TPJ62S	Bristol LHS6L		Eastern Coach Works	B35F	1977	Ex South Yorkshire, 1986
1607	TPJ64S	Bristol LHS6L		Eastern Coach Works	B35F	1977	Ex South Yorkshire, 1986
1610	WEX927S	Bristol LH6L		Eastern Coach Works	B43F	1977	Ex Tyne & Wear Omnibus, 1990
1611	WEX925S	Bristol LH6L		Eastern Coach Works	B43F	1977	Ex Tyne & Wear Omnibus, 1990

1614-1620

		Bristol LH6L		Eastern Coach Works	B43F	1978-80	Ex Tyne & Wear Omnibus, 1990

1614	AFB594V	1616	WEX928S	1618	DTL545T	1619	DTL548T	1620	YVL837S
1615	TTC787T	1617	WAE187T						

For the first time for many years, the two Busways open-toppers have seen regular use in service. The newer of the two, 1227 (SVK627G), wears Economic livery and has route branding on the upper deck advert panels. It was photographed during June 1993 outside Gypsies Green Stadium, South Shields. *David Little*

Following deregulation in 1986 Busways purchased a number of Bristol LHSs in order to introduce midibus routes. The only ones now in use are the examples from South Yorkshire PTE but new to London Country. No.1607 (TPJ64S), now in Blue Bus Services livery, is at Gallowgate, Newcastle during May 1993. *Keith Grimes*

Following the take-over of Tyne and Wear Omnibus by Busways that name and a modified livery was retained by Busways for use on midibuses. Recently the number of vehicles with this livery has been much reduced. Several Renault-Dodge midibuses carry this livery in Sunderland including 1630 (E630BVK) seen in March 1993 at the junction of Ryhope Road and Durham Road. *Phillip Stephenson*

1621-1640 — Renault-Dodge S56 — Alexander AM — B25F — 1987

1621	E621BVK	1625	E625BVK	1629	E629BVK	1633	E633BVK	1637	E637BVK
1622	E622BVK	1626	E626BVK	1630	E630BVK	1634	E634BVK	1638	E638BVK
1623	E623BVK	1627	E627BVK	1631	E631BVK	1635	E635BVK	1639	E639BVK
1624	E624BVK	1628	E628BVK	1632	E632BVK	1636	E636BVK	1640	E640BVK

1651-1662 — Iveco Daily 49-10 — Carlyle Dailybus 2 — B23F — 1988-89

1651	F651KNL	1654	F654KNL	1658	F658KNL	1659	F659KNL	1661	F661KNL
1653	F653KNL	1655	F655KNL						

1701	J701KCU	Dennis Dart 9.8SDL3017	Plaxton Pointer	B40F	1992
1702	J702KCU	Dennis Dart 9.8SDL3017	Plaxton Pointer	B40F	1992

1703-1743 — Dennis Dart 9.8SDL3017 — Alexander Dash — B40F — 1992-93

1703	K703PCN	1712	K712PCN	1720	K720PCN	1728	K728PNL	1736	L736VNL
1704	K704PCN	1713	K713PCN	1721	K721PCN	1729	L729VNL	1737	L737VNL
1705	K705PCN	1714	K714PCN	1722	K722PCN	1730	L730VNL	1738	L738VNL
1706	K706PCN	1715	K715PCN	1723	K723PNL	1731	L731VNL	1739	L739VNL
1707	K707PCN	1716	K716PCN	1724	K724PNL	1732	L732VNL	1740	L740VNL
1708	K708PCN	1717	K717PCN	1725	K725PNL	1733	L733VNL	1741	L741VNL
1709	K709PCN	1718	K718PCN	1726	K726PNL	1734	L734VNL	1742	L742VNL
1710	K710PCN	1719	K719PCN	1727	K727PNL	1735	L735VNL	1743	L743VNL
1711	K711PCN								

1744-1759 — Dennis Dart 9.8SDL3017 — Plaxton Pointer — B40F — 1993

1744	L744VNL	1748	L748VNL	1751	L751VNL	1754	L754VNL	1757	L757VNL
1745	L745VNL	1749	L749VNL	1752	L752VNL	1755	L755VNL	1758	L758VNL
1746	L746VNL	1750	L750VNL	1753	L753VNL	1756	L756VNL	1759	L759VNL

Like many other operators, Busways' newest vehicles have been Dennis Darts. The first two were supplied with Plaxton Pointer bodywork for the Blue Bus fleet. These were followed by a batch of twenty with Alexander Dash bodywork, an example of which is 1716 (K716PCN), seen outside Gallowgate Coach Station, Newcastle during May 1993. Additional orders have since increased the numbers to 41 Dash and 17 Pointers. It will be noted that the fleet number 1747 has not been used. *Keith Grimes*

1801	ECU201E	Bristol RESL6L	Eastern Coach Works	B45D	1967	Ex Bickers, 1988	
1802	TRY118H	Bristol RELL6L	Eastern Coach Works	B48F	1969	Ex Ipswich, 1988	

1810-1816

			Bristol RELL6L	Eastern Coach Works	B49F	1972-73	Ex Colchester, 1988
1810	YWC16L	1812	OWC720M	1814 OWC723M	1815 SWC25K	1816	SWC26K
1811	YWC18L	1813	OWC722M				

1817-1821

		Bristol RESL6G	Eastern Coach Works	B43F	1975	Ex Thamesdown, 1987
1817	JMW166P	1818 JMW167P	1819 JMW168P	1820 JMW169P	1821	JMW170P

1822	TDL567K	Bristol RELL6G	Eastern Coach Works	B53F	1971	Ex Catch a Bus, 1993
1823	AAH736J	Bristol RELL6G	Eastern Coach Works	B53F	1971	Ex Independent, Horsforth, 1993
1832	LBN201P	Leyland Leopard PSU3C/4R	Plaxton Elite III Express	C51F	1976	Ex Southend, 1988
1833	LBN202P	Leyland Leopard PSU3C/4R	Plaxton Elite III Express	C51F	1976	Ex Southend, 1988
1834	KTW438N	Leyland Leopard PSU3C/4R	Plaxton Elite III	C53F	1975	Ex Southend, 1988

1841-1850

			Leyland Leopard PSU3D/2R	Plaxton Derwent	B48F	1976	Ex GM Buses, 1987
1841	LTE486P	1843	LTE494P	1845 MTE14R	1847 MTE16R	1849	MTE18R
1842	LTE488P	1844	MTE13R	1846 MTE15R	1848 MTE17R	1850	MTE21R

1851	MTE32R	Leyland Leopard PSU3D/2R	Plaxton Derwent	B48F	1976	Ex GM Buses, 1990
1863	ESU263	Leyland Tiger TRCTL11/3R	Plaxton Paramount 3500	C51FT	1984	Ex Armchair, Brentford, 1992
1864	FYX824W	Leyland Leopard PSU3E/4R	Duple Dominant II Express	C49F	1980	Ex Grey-Green, London, 1988
1868	AHN388T	Leyland Leopard PSU3E/4R	Plaxton Supreme IV Express	DP55F	1978	Ex Cleveland Transit, 1990
1869	AHN389T	Leyland Leopard PSU3E/4R	Plaxton Supreme IV Express	DP55F	1978	Ex Cleveland Transit, 1990
1870	AHN390T	Leyland Leopard PSU3E/4R	Plaxton Supreme IV Express	DP55F	1978	Ex Cleveland Transit, 1990
1872	CMJ450T	Leyland Leopard PSU3E/4R	Plaxton Supreme III Express	C51F	1978	Ex Southend, 1988
1876	CBB476V	Leyland Leopard PSU3F/4R	Duple Dominant I	C47F	1980	
1877	CBB477V	Leyland Leopard PSU3F/4R	Duple Dominant I	C47F	1980	
1893	GBB993N	Leyland Leopard PSU3C/4R	Duple Dominant	C53F	1975	
1895	OTD824R	Leyland Leopard PSU3E/4R	Plaxton Supreme III Express	C51F	1977	Ex GM Buses, 1987
1896	OTD825R	Leyland Leopard PSU3E/4R	Plaxton Supreme III Express	C51F	1977	Ex GM Buses, 1987
1898	OTD827R	Leyland Leopard PSU3E/4R	Plaxton Supreme III Express	C51F	1977	Ex GM Buses, 1987

Liveries and allocations:

Armstrong Galley (Blue, yellow, orange and red): 3-9, 14-8, 31-4 (National Express livery), 51/5/6.

Blue Bus Services (Dark blue and cream): 61/3/5/6, 268/73/7, 303/12, 500/7/19/21/32/41-3/51/5, 1419/20/2/4/5/47/52, 1606/7/14/5/8/53/4/8/9, 1701/2, 1802/10-22/32/3/68-70/6/7/95/8.

Economic (Deep maroon and cream): 115/7/8/25/7, 270/1/4, 541-9/75/6, 1227.

Favourite (Orange, white and brown): 62, 71, 262, 374/81/6, 540/54/61/4, 1437/44, 1843/8/9/51/63/93/96.

Newcastle -Byker (Yellow, white and maroon): 314-63, 421-30, 601-6/8-19/84-97, 928-37, 1415/6/21/3/6-30/2-6/8-43/55, 1651/61, 1703-12.

Newcastle -Slatyford (Yellow, white and maroon): 204-15/7-9/21-3/44/7-61/3/94, 309/10, 413/4, 563/5, 620-40, 901-27/38, 1401-4/6/8-14/7/8, 1713-22, 1841/2/4-7/50.

South Shields (Yellow, white and blue): 116/9-24/6, 264-7/9/75/6/8-92/5/7-300, 301/2/4/68/9/75/6, 1405/7/31/45/6/8-51/3/4/6-60, 1801/72.

Sunderland (Yellow, white and green): 101-114, 378-80/4/5/8/90-7/9-405, 650-65/7-74/7-83, 800-839, 1218, 1621-33, 1723-8, 1864.

Reserve: 370/1/7/82/3/7/9/98, 509/44/56/58, 1604/5/10/1/6/7/9/20/55, 1834.

Previous registrations:

1JVK	F900JRG	HTY139W	FYX819W, KSU460	KSU462	D36YJN
2JVK	F715ENE	KSU454	B104DVK	KSU463	H133ACU
491JVX	F716ENE	KSU455	B105DVK	KSU464	H134ACU
552UTE	F717ENE	KSU456	B103DVK	KSU465	C155LJR
644HKX	E664JAV	KSU457	From New	KSU466	C103DYE
813VPU	G31WTY	KSU458	C110PCU	KTW438N	HU326, HWU72N
ESU263	A829PPP	KSU459	C109PCU	ONL645X	XMCN827X, 813VPU,
HTY137W	FYX820W, KSU464	KSU460	G32WTY		ONL450X, 813VPU
HTY138W	FYX821W, KSU463	KSU461	A751CRG		

Busways are a very keen operator of the Bristol RE and are still purchasing examples both for future service and as a source of spare parts. The former Thamesdown examples were the last Eastern Coach Works-bodied REs to be built and of these, 1820 (JMW169P), has had its dual-purpose seating replaced by bus seats. Bewick Street, opposite the Central Station, is the location of 1820 wearing Blue Bus Services livery. *Bill Potter*

Recently refurbished is Leyland Leopard 1833 (LBN202P) with Plaxton Elite Express body acquired from Southend in 1988. Wearing Blue Bus Services livery it is seen outside Newcastle Central Station while operating on a private hire. *Bill Potter*

Busways purchased a batch of Plaxton Derwent bodied Leyland Leopards from GM Buses in 1987. These vehicles are now operated by both Newcastle Busways and Favourite divisions. New to the Lancashire United fleet, 1849 (MTE18R) is seen in Sunderland operating service 14. *Steve Warburton*

Most of the midibuses are now in standard livery after repainting from the Tyne & Wear Omnibuses colours. Mercedes-Benz 1415 (D415TFT) is seen in Blackett Street, Newcastle. The City Busways fleetnames have since been replaced by Newcastle Busways following the amalgamation of the two divisions. *Phillip Stephenson*

CALVARY COACHES

K Rodham, Calvary Coaches, Victoria Road Garage, Concorde, Washington,
Tyne & Wear, NE37 2SY

HTC661	Bedford OB	SMT	C29F	1947	Ex Pinder, Morecambe, 1973
GUP647H	AEC Reliance 6MU3R	Plaxton Derwent	B55F	1969	Ex OK Travel, Bishop Auckland, 1992
NUP989J	Bedford YRQ	Duple Viceroy	C45F	1971	Ex Kingsley, Sunderland, 1989
FJR776L	Bedford YRT	Plaxton Elite III Express	C53F	1972	Ex Longstaff, Broomhill, 1989
XGR729R	Leyland National 11351A/1R		B49F	1977	Ex United, 1992
RBR86T	Bedford YMT	Willowbrook	B55F	1978	Ex Thornes, Bubwith, 1993
B207GNL	Ford Transit 160	Alexander AM	DP16F	1985	Ex Metro Taxis, 1990
B200GNL	Ford Transit 160	Alexander AM	DP16F	1985	Ex Metro Taxis, 1991
E901DRG	Bedford YRQ	Plaxton Elite III Express	C45F	1988	Ex Bob Smith, Langley Park, 1990

Livery: Two tone blue and cream

Previous Registrations:
RBR86T   XKU229T, HBT378S

After serving the OK fleet for 20 years, Plaxton Derwent-bodied AEC Reliance GUP647H joined the fleet of Calvary Coaches in 1992. It is normally used on the service from Washington to Tynemouth, but was photographed outside the Central Station in Newcastle while on a private hire. *David Little*

CATCH A BUS

Hylton Castle Motors Ltd, Station Approach, East Boldon, Tyne & Wear, NE36 0AB

Reg	Chassis	Body		Type	Year	History
YFM269L	Bristol RELL6G	Eastern Coach Works		B50F	1973	Ex Crosville Wales, 1988
YFM283L	Bristol RELL6G	Eastern Coach Works		B50F	1973	Ex Crosville Wales, 1988
HIL4346	Leyland Atlantean AN68/2R	East Lancs Sprint (1992)		B46F	1974	Ex Yorkshire Rider, 1992
HIL4349	Leyland Atlantean AN68/2R	East Lancs Sprint (1992)		B46F	1974	Ex Yorkshire Rider, 1992
GCL347N	Bristol RELH6L(6HLX)	Eastern Coach Works		DP49F	1974	Ex Cambus, 1989
ORC416N	Bristol RELH6G	Eastern Coach Works		B53F	1974	Ex Trent, 1990
ORC417N	Bristol RELH6G	Eastern Coach Works		B53F	1974	Ex Trent, 1990
GTX359N	Bristol RESL6G	Eastern Coach Works		B47F	1974	Ex Williams, Cross Keys, 1989
GTX361N	Bristol RESL6G	Eastern Coach Works		B47F	1975	Ex Williams, Cross Keys, 1989
HIL2147	Leyland Leopard PSU3C/4R	Duple Dominant E		DP53F	1975	Ex Wimpey, 1991
HIL2148	Leyland Leopard PSU3C/4R	Duple Dominant E		DP53F	1976	Ex Wimpey, 1991
HIL2141	Leyland Leopard PSU3D/4R	Plaxton Derwent II (1991)		B51F	1977	Ex Ceramia Parties, 1990
HIL2142	Leyland Leopard PSU3E/4R	Plaxton Derwent II (1991)		B51F	1977	Ex Go-Ahead Northern, 1990
AIW257	DAF MB200DKL600	Plaxton Supreme III		C53F	1978	Ex Harris, West Thurrock, 1986
KRN112T	Leyland Leopard PSU3E/4R	Duple Dominant II		C47F	1979	Ex Brownrigg, Egremont, 1992
KRN117T	Leyland Leopard PSU3E/4R	Duple Dominant II		DP49F	1979	Ex Brownrigg, Egremont, 1992
TUP572V	Leyland Leopard PSU3E/4R	Plaxton Derwent II (1992)		B51F	1980	Ex Go-Ahead Northern, 1991
OYS349V	AEC Reliance 6U3ZR	Duple Dominant		B53F	1980	Ex Hutchison, Overtown, 1988
NPD689W	Leyland Leopard PSU3E/4R	Duple Dominant		B53F	1981	Ex Safeguard, Guildford, 1992
TPA968X	Leyland Leopard PSU3F/4R	Duple Dominant		B53F	1981	Ex Safeguard, Guildford, 1992
HIL2143	Leyland Leopard PSU3F/4R	Plaxton Derwent II (1991)		B51F	1982	Ex Go-Ahead Northern, 1991
HIL2144	Leyland Leopard PSU3F/4R	Plaxton Derwent II (1991)		B51F	1982	Ex Go-Ahead Northern, 1991
LFT93X	Leyland Leopard PSU3F/4R	Plaxton Derwent II (1992)		B51F	1982	Ex Go-Ahead Northern, 1991
HIL2145	Leyland Leopard PSU3F/4R	Willowbrook 003		C49F	1982	Ex Potteries, 1986
HIL2146	Leyland Leopard PSU3G/2R	Duple Dominant		B49F	1982	Ex Merthyr Tydfil, 1989
HIL6462	Bova EL26/581	Bova Europa		C53F	1983	Ex The Londoners, 1983
HCC49	Bova FHD12.280	Bova Futura		C49FT	1984	
FDZ8195	Volvo B10M-61	Van Hool Alizée		C53F	1984	Ex Shearings, 1990
FDZ1635	Volvo B10M-61	Van Hool Alizée		C53F	1984	Ex Shearings, 1990
HIL6461	Volvo B10M-61	Van Hool Alizée		C53F	1985	Ex Shearings, 1992
F166XCS	Mercedes-Benz 609D	Scott		C24F	1989	Ex Clyde Coast, Ardrossan, 1990
F810OCN	Mercedes-Benz 609D	Reeve Burgess Beaver		B20F	1989	
K831SFT	Dennis Dart 9.8SDL3017	Plaxton Pointer		B40F	1993	
K832SFT	Dennis Dart 9.8SDL3017	Plaxton Pointer		B40F	1993	

Livery: White with red, orange and yellow; overall advert - HIL4346, HIL4349.

Previous Registrations:

AIW257	XVW453S, MIA626	HIL2143	LFT91X	HIL2148	MTV761P
FDZ8195	A174MNE	HIL2144	LFT92X	HIL4346	SUG561M
FDZ1635	A173MNE	HIL2145	VFA69X	HIL4349	SUG595M
HCC49	A212DBB	HIL2146	OWO233Y	HIL6461	B488UNB
HIL2141	OKY52R	HIL2147	LAL748P	HIL6462	YMV352Y
HIL2142	VPT169R				

To replace Leyland Nationals, Catch A Bus obtained a number of Bristol REs, all with the Eastern Coach Works body, an interesting reversal of the vehicles' historic rôles. Even today, seven remain for use on the South Shields town services. YFM269L was new to Crosville with dual-purpose seating, the bus seats now having been fitted by Catch A Bus.
Mike Fowler

Catch A Bus have had six Leyland Leopard chassis fitted with Plaxton Derwent bodies replacing Willowbrook or Duple coachwork. HIL2144 was originally Northern's LFT92X and in this May 1993 view is entering Sunderland's Central bus station on service 6 from South Shields.
Keith Grimes

During 1992 a pair of Leyland Atlantean chassis were obtained from Yorkshire Rider and rebodied with single deck Sprint bodies by East Lancashire. HIL4349 which was re-registered from SUG595M, is seen in Kepple Street, South Shields. Both vehicles carry identical advertising liveries for Hylton Castle's own activities. *Mike Fowler*

Apart from a midibus the first new vehicles to join the Catch A Bus fleet were a pair of Dennis Darts with Plaxton Pointer bodywork. Fowler Street, South Shields is the location for K832SFT operating South Shields local service 48 to Brockley Whins, one of the Darts' regular duties.
Mike Fowler

CLASSIC COACHES

Classic Coaches (Continental) Ltd, Classic House, Morrison Road, Annfield Plain,
Co. Durham, DH9 7RX

MGR656P	Bristol LH6L	Eastern Coach Works	B43F	1975	Ex Parker, Sunderland, 1992
SFV206P	Leyland Leopard PSU5A/4R	Plaxton Supreme III	C48FT	1976	Ex Wreake Valley, 1990
JJG12P	Leyland Atlantean AN68/1R	Eastern Coach Works	H44/31F	1976	Ex Bedlington & District, 1993
WRO448S	Leyland Leopard PSU3E/4R	Plaxton Supreme III	C48F	1977	
ANC906T	Leyland Atlantean AN68A/1R	Park Royal	H43/32F	1978	Ex GM Buses, 1993
ANC923T	Leyland Atlantean AN68A/1R	Park Royal	H43/32F	1978	Ex GM Buses, 1993
BNC950T	Leyland Atlantean AN68A/1R	Park Royal	H43/32F	1978	Ex GM Buses, 1993
NGR116T	Leyland Leopard PSU5C/4R	Plaxton Supreme III	C50F	1979	Ex Hardwick, Scarborough, 1989
LCY110X	Leyland Leopard PSU3F/4R	Willowbrook 003	C46F	1982	Ex Eagre, Morton, 1993
ONL648X	Volvo B58-61	Duple Dominant IV	C53F	1982	Ex Swan Hunter, Wallsend, 1992
MSL62X	Leyland Tiger TRCTL11/3R	Plaxton Supreme VI	C48FT	1982	Ex Midland, Auchterarder, 1992
325CCE	Leyland Tiger TRCTL11/3R	Plaxton Viewmaster	C49FT	1982	Ex Williams, Brecon, 1991
656CCE	Volvo B10M-61	Jonckheere Jubilee P90	CH51/9FT	1983	Ex Bleanch, Hetton, 1992
VOI9752	Volvo B10M-61	Caetano Algarve	C53F	1986	Ex Scarlet Band, West Cornforth, 1992
VDM175	Volvo B10M-61	Van Hool Alizée	C49FT	1986	Ex Scarlet Band, West Cornforth, 1992
625FYO	Volvo B10M-61	Plaxton Paramount 3500 III	C49FT	1987	Ex Wray, Harrogate, 1992
593CCE	Volvo B10M-61	Caetano Algarve	C49FT	1987	Ex SB Travel, Redcar, 1993
956CCE	DAF SBR3000DKZ570	Plaxton Paramount 4000 III	CH53/18CT	1988	Ex Park's, Hamilton, 1991
F95CBD	Volvo B10M-60	Jonckheere Deauville P599	C50FT	1989	Ex Antler, Rugeley, 1990
F418LNL	Volvo B10M-61	Ikarus Blue Danube	C49FT	1989	
G500CVC	Volvo B10M-53	Van Hool Alizée	C49FT	1990	Ex Harry Shaw, Coventry, 1993
G700CRW	Volvo B10M-50	Van Hool Alizée	C49FT	1990	Ex Harry Shaw, Coventry, 1993
K729GBE	Mercedes-Benz 814D	Autobus Classique	C25F	1993	

Livery: Red, maroon and gold.

Previous Registrations:

325CCE	THN882X, 226DMW, JFO108X	KSU479	D526BBV
593CCE	E500KEF	ONL648X	TND130X, LIB6349
625FYO	D951MWX	MSL64X	FGD824X, 913EWC
656CCE	A316XHE	VDM175	From new
956CCE	E314AGA	VOI9752	C679KDS

Classic Coaches started to operate local services during 1992 and have caused much reaction by United as well as Go-Ahead Northern and its subsidiaries. One such service runs from Newcastle Worswick Street to Durham. MGR656P, having worked for several owners, stands at the top of Worswick Street. The Classic livery of red and maroon stands out and recent double decker arrivals operate as Classic Liners.
Steve Warburton

COUSINS COACHES

J Cousins, 59a Swinside Drive, Belmont, Co Durham, DH1 1AF

AJB181A	Bedford YRQ	Plaxton Elite II	C41F	1972	Ex Witherwack YC, Sunderland, 1990
HPY317N	Ford A0609	Northern Counties	DP20F	1975	Ex Lancaster, 1990
NOD215P	Bedford YMT	Duple Dominant	C53F	1976	Ex Cheesey, Meadowfield, 1991
VFP321S	Ford A0609	Moseley Faro	DP25F	1977	Ex Smith, Somercotes, 1989
AND700Y	Ford Transit 160	Deansgate	M12	1982	Ex Deansgate demonstrator, 1985
D418NBE	Mercedes-Benz L307D	Coachcraft	M16	1986	
D606JWR	Renault Master T35D	Coachcraft	M12	1986	Ex West End, Leamington, 1988
D360SNS	Freight Rover Sherpa	Scott	C21F	1987	Ex West, Stockton, 1993
E52CVK	Ford Transit VE6	Dormobile	B16F	1987	
E218PWY	Volkswagen LT55	Optare City Pacer	B25F	1987	Ex Yorkshire Rider, 1991
F223GTY	Bedford Midi	Bristol Street	M13	1988	
F598TEE	Mercedes-Benz 609D	Coachcraft	C20F	1988	

Livery: White and orange

Previous Registrations:
AJB181A   EOR559K

Cousins Coaches operate a number of Durham County Council services from Chester-le-Street using a variety of mini and midi buses. South Burns, Chester-le-Street is the setting for Dormobile-bodied Ford Transit E52CVK. There seems to be confusion as to which service the vehicle is operating! *David Little*

DARLINGTON TRANSPORT

Darlington Transport Co Ltd, Haughton Road Bus Depot, Haughton Road,
Darlington, Co Durham, DL1 1SN

1-6

				Ward Dalesman GRXI		Wadham Stringer Vanguard	B48D	1983	
1	A101CVN	3	A103CVN	4	A104CVN	5	A105CVN	6	A106CVN
2	A102CVN								

9	KIW5939	Leyland Leopard PSU5D/4R	Plaxton Supreme V	C50F	1981	Ex Wallace Arnold, 1987
10	KIW5940	Leyland Leopard PSU5D/4R	Plaxton Supreme V	C50F	1981	Ex Wallace Arnold, 1987
13	GHN813V	Dennis Dominator SD128A	Marshall Camair 80	B46D	1980	
20	GHN820V	Dennis Dominator SD128A	Marshall Camair 80	B46D	1980	
21	VRM621S	Leyland Leopard PSU3E/4R	Duple Dominant II Express	C49F	1979	Ex Cumberland, 1986
22	VRM622S	Leyland Leopard PSU3E/4R	Duple Dominant II Express	C49F	1979	Ex Kettlewell, Retford, 1986
23	KRN110T	Leyland Leopard PSU3E/4R	Duple Dominant II Express	C49F	1979	Ex Cumberland, 1986
24	KRN115T	Leyland Leopard PSU3E/4R	Duple Dominant II Express	C49F	1979	Ex Cumberland, 1986
25	F725MNB	Ford Transit 190	Mellor	M14	1989	
26	GPH1V	Volvo B58-56	Duple Dominant II Express	C53F	1980	
27	H427DVM	Leyland DAF 400	Made-to-Measure	M16	1990	Ex Kentish Bus, 1990
28	HTV18V	Volvo B58-61	Plaxton Supreme IV	C57F	1980	Ex Skill, Nottingham, 1991
29	GPH2V	Volvo B58-56	Duple Dominant II Express	C53F	1980	Ex Palmer, Carlisle, 1992

31-36

				MCW Metrorider MF154/9		MCW	DP33F	1988	
31	E31NEF	33	E33NEF	34	E34NEF	35	E35NEF	36	E36NEF
32	E32NEF								

37	L837MWT	Optare MetroRider	Optare	B31F	1993	
38	L838MWT	Optare MetroRider	Optare	B31F	1993	
39	L839MWT	Optare MetroRider	Optare	B31F	1993	
40	L840MWT	Optare MetroRider	Optare	B31F	1993	

50-60

				Daimler Fleetline SRG6LX-36		Roe	B48D	1972	
50	NHN250K	52	NHN252K	56	NHN256K	58	NHN258K	60	NHN260K
51	NHN251K	55	NHN255K	57	NHN257K	59	NHN259K		

69	PHN569R	Leyland Leopard PSU3D/2R	Duple Dominant	DP49D	1976	
70	PHN570R	Leyland Leopard PSU3D/2R	Duple Dominant	DP53F	1976	
71	PHN571R	Leyland Leopard PSU3D/2R	Duple Dominant	DP49D	1976	
72	PHN572R	Leyland Leopard PSU3D/2R	Duple Dominant	DP53F	1976	
104	1624WY	Volvo B10M-61	Plaxton Paramount 3500	C53F	1983	Ex Wallace Arnold, 1988
105	4695WY	Volvo B10M-61	Plaxton Paramount 3500	C53F	1983	Ex Wallace Arnold, 1988
108	3148WY	Volvo B10M-61	Plaxton Paramount 3500	C53F	1983	Ex Wallace Arnold, 1988
116	PJT516W	Ford R1114	Plaxton Supreme IV	C53F	1985	Ex Watson, Hurworth Pl, 1989
118	OBR908P	Ford R1114	Duple Dominant	C53F	1984	Ex Watson, Hurworth Pl, 1989
119	B99COO	Ford R1115	Plaxton Paramount 3200	C35F	1985	Ex Hornsby, Ashby, 1989
121	GUB151Y	Bedford YMT	Plaxton Paramount 3200	C51F	1983	Ex Rydal, Richmond, 1989
125	A745ERM	Bedford YNT	Duple Laser	C53F	1984	Ex Rydal, Richmond, 1989
201	PAU201R	Daimler Fleetline CRG6LX	Northern Counties	H47/30D	1976	Ex Nottingham, 1990
202	PAU202R	Daimler Fleetline CRG6LX	Northern Counties	H47/30D	1976	Ex Nottingham, 1990
205	PAU205R	Daimler Fleetline CRG6LX	Northern Counties	H47/30D	1976	Ex Nottingham, 1990
206	PAU206R	Daimler Fleetline CRG6LX	Northern Counties	H47/30D	1976	Ex Nottingham, 1990
208	PAU208R	Daimler Fleetline CRG6LX	Northern Counties	H47/30D	1976	Ex Nottingham, 1991
209	PAU209R	Daimler Fleetline CRG6LX	Northern Counties	H47/30D	1976	Ex Nottingham, 1992

Liveries: Blue and cream
Overall advertisements: 3
Previous operators colours: 9, 10, 104/5/8/19/21/5

Previous Registrations:

1624WY	FUA382Y	4695WY	FUA384Y	KIW5940	PNW340W
3148WY	FUA383Y	KIW5939	PNW339W		

The most unusual vehicles in the Darlington fleet are six of the rare Ward Dalesman chassis, here bodied by Wadham Stringer. These were the only rear-engined Dalesmen built, the other twelve being underfloor-engined coaches. Photographed while approaching Darlington Market Place when operating service 1 to Red Hall is 2 (A102CVN). *Bill Potter*

Only one batch of MCW Metroriders has been purchased by Darlington although some of the Optare version are due for early delivery. Awaiting passengers are left in no doubt that 34 (E34NEF) is a 'No Smoking Bus'. *Bill Potter*

Darlington purchased two batches of Dennis Dominators with Marshall Camair bodywork. 13 (GHN813V), seen approaching Darlington Market Place, is one of two survivors in the fleet. *Keith Grimes*

The Darlington fleet contains four former Cumberland express coaches. All are Leyland Leopards with Duple Dominant II bodywork, two originating in the Ribble fleet. These are mainly used on services out of the borough, such as the 38 from Richmond to Catterick. No.22 is seen amid stone-faced buildings typical of the area. *Steve Warburton*

Now in its twenty-first year, Daimler Fleetline 59 (NHN259K) was photographed in Tubwell Row, Darlington during May 1993. Vehicles from this batch are now being refurbished for further service while much younger Dennis Dominators are being withdrawn.
Keith Grimes

London Country used a pair of Volvo B58 express coaches with Duple Dominant bodywork in 1980 for evaluation as possible replacements for the AEC Reliance. Darlington purchased GPH1V in 1990 and this was re-united with its sister, GPH2V in 1992. Carrying route branding for X77 Darlington - Metro Centre - Newcastle, 26 (GPH1V) is leaving Darlington for its northern destination.

Phillip Stephenson

Darlington re-introduced double deckers into the fleet in 1990 when a batch of Daimler Fleetlines were purchased. To combat competition with newcomer, Your Bus, Darlington are operating these vehicles with a conductor. No.205 (PAU205R), new to Nottingham and fitted with Northern Counties bodywork to Nottingham's design, is seen near Darlington Market Place.
Bill Potter

DELTA

Delta Coaches Ltd, Blue House, Point Road, Portrack, Stockton-on-Tees,
Cleveland, TS18 2PJ

IIL3710	Bristol RELL6G	Eastern Coach Works	B53F	1969	Ex Wood, Great Longstone, 1990
UEL566J	Bristol RELL6G	Eastern Coach Works	B50F	1970	Ex Cumbrae, Millport, 1988
IIL2271	Bristol RELL6G	Eastern Coach Works	B53F	1971	Ex Excelsior, Telford, 1988
YHU513J	Bristol RELL6L(6HLX)	Eastern Coach Works	B53F	1971	Ex Kemp, Clacton, 1991
EPW513K	Bristol RELL6G	Eastern Coach Works	B53F	1972	Ex Eastern Counties, 1988
XLJ729K	Bristol RELL6G	Eastern Coach Works	B50F	1972	Ex Wilts & Dorset, 1991
LTG38L	Bristol RESL6L(6HLX)	Eastern Coach Works	B44F	1972	Ex Parfitt's, Rhymney Bridge, 1992
NAT934A	Leyland Leopard PSU3B/4R	Duple Dominant	C49F	1972	Ex Southdown, 1986
IIL1839	Bristol RELL6G	Eastern Coach Works	B53F	1972	Ex North Devon, 1986
LHT166L	Bristol RELL6L	Eastern Coach Works	B50F	1973	Ex Stephenson, Rochford, 1993
NWU321M	Bristol RELL6G	Eastern Coach Works	B53F	1973	Ex North Devon, 1986
HTG355N	Bristol RESL6L	Eastern Coach Works	B44F	1975	Ex Parfitt's, Rhymney Bridge, 1992
PVB803S	Leyland Leopard PSU3E/4R	Duple Dominant II	C49F	1978	Ex Thorpe, Harbury, 1991
YNF347T	Bedford YMT	Plaxton Supreme III	C53F	1979	Ex Parnham, Ludgershall, 1992
DNY535V	Leyland Leopard PSU4E/2R	Marshall	B45F	1980	Ex Islwyn, 1991
HIL6581	Volvo B10M-61	Jonckheere Jubilee P50	C49FT	1982	Ex Jason, St Mary Cray, 1992
FIL8694	Leyland Tiger TRCTL11/3R	Padane ZX	C47F	1982	Ex Crescent, North Walsham, 1992
HIL6580	Volvo B10M-61	Duple Dominant III	C51FT	1982	Ex Prindale, Barwick-in-Elmet, 1988
HIL6587	Leyland Royal Tiger	Plaxton Paramount 3500	C53F	1984	Ex Farrow, Melton Mowbray, 1992
ILL1840	Volvo B10M-61	LAG Galaxy	C49FT	1984	Ex Bleanch, Hetton, 1992
C565TUT	Ford Transit 190	Dormobile	B16F	1986	Ex Midland Fox, 1988
E811UHF	Mercedes-Benz 811D	Coachcraft	C24F	1987	Ex Neal, Chippenham, 1993
HIL6755	Volvo B10M-61	Plaxton Paramount 3500 III	C49FT	1988	Ex Dodsworth, Boroughbridge, 1993
F231OFP	Volvo B10M-61	Duple 320	C53F	1988	Ex Oriel, Enstone, 1990

Livery: Red and grey (buses); white, red and blue (coaches)

Previous Registrations:

FIL8694	XPP289X	IIL1839	TWX198L
HIL6580	FHS726X, GSV903, XVU917X	IIL2271	BVF668J
HIL6581	ENV828X, 674SHY, ORL374X	IIL3710	EFM179H
HIL6587	A851UYM	IIL1840	A231GNR
HIL6755	E711TYG	NAT934A	CUF259L

One of four Neoplans with Plaxton Paramount 4000 bodywork in the Durham Travel fleet is 20 (RIB4320). Sunderland Park Lane bus station is the setting as it operates on National Express Rapide service 526 to London Victoria. *Phillip Stephenson*

While the main part of its business is National Express work, Durham Travel has built up a substantial private hire business. Plaxton-bodied Scania K113CRB (J16DTS), however, is seen in Oxford Street, London on National Express Rapide service 529 to Durham. *Colin Lloyd*

THE EDEN

Eden Bus Services Ltd, Eden Garage, West Auckland, Co Durham, DL14 9JY

L12	PPT445P	Leyland Leopard PSU3C/4R	Plaxton Derwent	B55F	1976	
L14	PPT446P	Leyland Leopard PSU3C/4R	Plaxton Derwent	B55F	1976	
L16	FGR474S	Leyland Leopard PSU3E/4R	Duple Dominant II	C51F	1978	
L17	JGR416T	Leyland Leopard PSU3E/4R	Duple Dominant II	C51F	1978	
L18	KBR933T	Leyland Leopard PSU3E/4R	Plaxton Supreme III Express	C51F	1978	
L19	LPT972T	Leyland Leopard PSU3E/4R	Duple Dominant II	C53F	1979	
L20	OGR893T	Leyland Leopard PSU3E/4R	Duple Dominant II	C53F	1979	
L21	RGR756V	Leyland Leopard PSU3E/4R	Duple Dominant II	C51F	1979	
L22	TUP921V	Leyland Leopard PSU3E/4R	Duple Dominant II	C53F	1979	
L23	VUP731V	Leyland Leopard PSU3E/4R	Duple Dominant II	C53F	1980	
L24	KPT169N	Leyland Leopard PSU3B/4R	Plaxton Elite III Express	DP53F	1980	Ex Trimdon MS, 1982
L25	GNL843N	Leyland Leopard PSU3B/4R	Alexander AY	DP47F	1975	Ex Gillingham, Annfield Plain 1984
L26	KFL199P	Leyland Leopard PSU3C/4R	Plaxton Elite III Express	C51F	1975	Ex Burdett, Mosborough, 1987
LT1	369EBC	Leyland Tiger TRCTL11/3R	Plaxton Paramount 3200 E	C48FT	1983	
MR1	F201RVN	MCW MetroRider MF154	MCW	DP31F	1988	
MR2	F202RVN	MCW MetroRider MF154	MCW	DP31F	1988	
MR3	F203RVN	MCW MetroRider MF154	MCW	DP31F	1988	
R1	F851BUA	Renault-Dodge S56	Northern Counties	B24F	1988	Ex Rider York, 1992
R2	F363BUA	Renault-Dodge S56	Northern Counties	B24F	1988	Ex Rider York, 1992
S1	D68YRF	Freight Rover Sherpa 374	Dormobile	B16F	1986	Ex Midland Red North, 1990
S2	D70YRF	Freight Rover Sherpa 374	Dormobile	B16F	1986	Ex Midland Red North, 1990
V1	LTN753X	Volvo B58-56	Duple Dominant III	C53F	1981	

Livery: Ivory and red

Previous Registrations:
369EBC   TTY841Y

Still giving yeoman service are the two Leyland Leopard/Plaxton Derwent buses which were new in 1976. The second of the pair, PPT446P, is laying-over on Spennymoor High Street, the terminus of many services since the closure of the bus station. *J Carter*

About to enter Bishop Auckland bus station LTN753X, The Eden's only Volvo, displays its Duple Dominant III bodywork clearly. This general style of bodywork is more associated with Anglo-Scottish motorway journeys of the dimming past, rather than local bus work on which it was being used when photographed in May 1993. *Keith Grimes*

Until 1992, GNL843N was fitted with 62 bus seats in a three and two arrangement. Now equipped with 47 coach seats it is seen in Tubwell Row, Darlington. *Keith Grimes*

Three long-wheelbase MCW Metroriders joined The Eden fleet in 1988. The first of the three, F201RVN, was photographed about to enter Bishop Auckland bus station. It was operating on service 91, which serves the former railway town of Shildon, en route to Darlington. *John Carter*

ERB

E Brown, Hannington Place, Byker Bridge, Newcastle-upon-Tyne,
Tyne & Wear, NE6 1JT

A1	E246RBE	Mercedes-Benz L307D	Coachcraft	M12	1988	Ex Dalesman, Ilkley, 1990
A3	D550VVV	Ford Transit 190	Dormobile	DP16F	1986	Ex Gibbs, Milton Keynes, 1989
B1	D884WTY	Mercedes-Benz 609D	Devon Conversions	DP18FL	1987	Ex Jumbulance Project, Newcastle, 1991
B2	E857ETY	Mercedes-Benz 609D	Reeve Burgess Beaver	DP24F	1988	
B3	F108MVK	Mercedes-Benz 609D	Reeve Burgess Beaver	DP23F	1989	
	F988TNV	Mercedes-Benz 407D	Reeve Burgess	M15	1989	Ex Phoenix, Blyth, 1991
C1	G496HSX	Mercedes-Benz 811D	PMT Ami	DP33F	1990	Ex McIlwraith, Bailieston, 1991
C2	G665OVO	Mercedes-Benz 814D	Reeve Burgess Beaver	DP33F	1990	Ex Ace, Mansfield, 1992
	H856NOC	Iveco Daily 49.10	Carlyle Dailybus 2	B21F	1991	Ex Carlyle demonstrator, 1992

Livery: Maroon and cream

ERB Services operate a number of Tyne and Wear tendered routes in the Newcastle and Gateshead areas using a variety of mini and midi buses. One service which penetrates the centre of Newcastle is service 6 operating between Central Station and Jesmond Vale. Dormobile-bodied Ford Transit D550VVV is seen at the junction of Grainger Street and Market Street, Newcastle. *Bill Potter*

FAIRLEY'S

R Fairley, Unit 13, Tudhoe Industrial Estate, Tudhoe, Co Durham

PRH251G	Leyland Atlantean PDR1A/1	Roe	H44/33F	1969	Ex Kingston-upon-Hull, 1992
WWH63L	Daimler Fleetline CRG6LXB	Northern Counties	H43/32F	1973	Ex Wray, Harrogate, 1990
NUN518R	Ford R1114	Duple Dominant	C53F	1977	Ex MacArthur, Ardrishaig, 1990
4796EL	Volvo B10M-61	Van Hool Astral	CH47/11FT	1984	Ex Ellerby, Wolsingham, 1990
C903JET	Mercedes-Benz L608D	Reeve Burgess	C19F	1986	Ex Davison, Wingate, 1991
E891VWL	Volvo B10M-60	Ikarus Blue Danube	C49FT	1987	Ex McLean, Carterton, 1991
F434XDC	Mercedes-Benz L609D	Coachcraft	C24F	1989	

Livery: White and brown

Previous Registrations:
4796EL   A904JEF

Fairley's now operate two double decks, a former Hull Leyland Atlantean with Roe bodywork and this Daimler Fleetline with Northern Counties. WWH63L, carrying a now rare 'WH' index mark, received its non-standard front panel when owned by Ashville College, Harrogate. *Bill Potter*

GARDINERS

Gardiner Bros Ltd, 19 Coulson Street, Spennymoor, Co Durham, DL16 7RS

Reg	Chassis	Body	Seats	Year	Notes
SPT722V	Volvo B58-56	Duple Dominant II	C53F	1979	
JVF819V	Leyland Leopard PSU3E/4R	Plaxton Supreme IV Express	C49F	1979	Ex Cambus, 1992
GRF265V	Leyland Leopard PSU3E/4R	Duple Dominant II	C53F	1979	Ex Brownrigg, Egremont, 1992
VGR571V	Volvo B58-56	Plaxton Supreme IV Express	C53F	1980	
XBR371V	Volvo B58-61	Plaxton Supreme IV	C57F	1980	
TPT23V	Leyland Leopard PSU3E/4R	Willowbrook 003	C49F	1980	Ex Northumbria, 1991
YVY8V	Volvo B58-61	Duple Dominant II	C57F	1980	Ex Grierson, Fishburn, 1988
VNH169W	Leyland Leopard PSU3F/4R	Duple Dominant IV Express	C49F	1981	Ex Green, Kirkintilloch, 1991
MAP351W	Leyland Leopard PSU3F/4R	Plaxton Supreme IV Express	C48F	1981	Ex Green, Kirkintilloch, 1991
WDO759	Volvo B10M-61	Plaxton Paramount 3500 II	C48FT	1985	Ex Excelsior, Bournemouth, 1988
D895VAO	Mercedes-Benz L609D	Reeve Burgess	B20F	1986	Ex Classic, Annfield Plain, 1993
WBB962	Volvo B10M-61	Plaxton P'mount 3200 (1990)	C57F	1987	Ex Wilson, Carnwath, 1989
UFE712	Volvo B10M-61	Plaxton Paramount 3500 III	C51FT	1987	
F830XAJ	Volvo B10M-60	Van Hool Alizée	C55F	1989	
G702BEF	Volvo B10M-60	Van Hool Alizée	C51FT	1989	
G917GTG	Mercedes-Benz 811D	Optare StarRider	B33F	1989	Ex Stonehouse Coaches, 1992
G955WNR	Leyland Swift LBM6T/2RA	Reeve Burgess Harrier	B39F	1989	Ex Green, Kirkintilloch, 1991
G965WNR	Leyland Swift ST2R44C97A4	Reeve Burgess Harrier	B39F	1989	Ex Green, Kirkintilloch, 1991

Livery: White, orange and brown.

Previous Registrations:

UFE712	E491HHN	WDO759	B900SPR, 21MMM, B618UPR
WBB962	D960HMS		

Gardiners now operate services to many places in County Durham including Bishop Auckland, Chester-le-Street, Spennymoor and Durham City using a mixture of midibuses and coaches. Optare StarRider G917GTG, with its third owner in four years, is entering Bishop Auckland bus station on a town service in May 1993. Bishop Auckland has not yet achieved 'City' status as the blind implies. *Keith Grimes*

GARNETTS

L Garnett, Unit E1 Romanway Industrial Estate, Tindale Crescent,
Co Durham, DL14 9AW

NGB84M	Leyland Atlantean AN68/2R	Alexander AL	H45/29F	1973	Ex Rennie, Dunfermline, 1991
GNS669N	Leyland Atlantean AN68/2R	Alexander AL	H45/31F	1975	Ex Rennie, Dunfermline, 1991
NEL113P	Leyland Leopard PSU3E/4R	Plaxton Supreme III Express	C53F	1976	Ex Highway, Portsmouth, 1993
XUP404R	Ford R1114	Plaxton Supreme III	C53F	1977	Ex Ellerby, Wolsingham, 1990
VFT190T	Leyland Atlantean AN68/2R	MCW	H49/37F	1979	Ex Go-Ahead Northern, 1992
DWK418T	Ford R1114	Plaxton Supreme IV	C53F	1979	Ex J & C, Newton Aycliffe, 1991
YNL213V	Leyland Atlantean AN68A/2R	MCW	H49/37F	1979	Ex Go-Ahead Northern, 1991
FHS750X	Volvo B10M-61	Duple Goldliner III	C53F	1982	Ex Weir, Clydebank, 1992
DJI1594	Bova FHD12.280	Bova Futura	C49FT	1984	Ex J & C, Newton Aycliffe, 1991
MKH82E	Leyland Tiger TRCTL11/3R	Plaxton Paramount 3500	C48FT	1984	Ex Boro'line, 1992
8087WE	Bova FHD12.280	Bova Futura	C49FT	1986	Ex Hurst & Leak, Goose Green, 1992
H711BRG	Toyota Coaster HDB30R	Caetano Optimo II	C21F	1990	

Livery: White, red and yellow

Previous Registrations:

8087WE	B210PDC, WSV570, B815KCU	MKH82E	A123MBA
DJI1594	A771HPY		

Garnett's of Tindale Crescent operates four double deck buses, mainly on school contracts. Of these two are former Tyne and Wear PTE Atlanteans with MCW bodies while the other pair are former Greater Glasgow Atlanteans with that operator's standard Alexander bodywork. YNL213V is seen outside Bishop Auckland bus station while operating a school contract. *Keith Grimes*

GEORGE BELL

G Bell, 35 Lord Street, New Silksworth, Sunderland, Tyne & Wear.

Depot: Pallion Quay, Pallion, Sunderland.

UPP268R	Bristol LHL6L	Plaxton Supreme III	C53F	1978	Ex Star Travel, Dipton, 1992
OWG258X	Leyland Cub CU435	Reeve Burgess	B33F	1982	Ex Silverwing, Keynsham, 1993
A850UYM	Leyland Royal Tiger B54	Plaxton Paramount 3500	C53F	1984	Ex Smith's, Sittingbourne, 1990
FIB5668	Volvo B10M-61	Duple Caribbean 2	C49FT	1986	Ex Swanbrook, Cheltenham, 1989
D557KNW	Iveco Daily 49.10	Robin Hood City Nippy	DP21F	1986	Ex Merseybus, 1993

Livery: White and blue

Previous Registrations:

FIB5668	C119XDD	UPP268R	PTM53R, 617MUR

George Bell uses two vehicles on stage service, an Iveco with Robin Hood bodywork, and a Leyland Cub with a Reeve Burgess design. Both coachbuilders, unfortunately, are now confined to history - albeit a fairly recent one. The latter vehicle, OWG258X was photographed leaving Sunderland central bus station. The angular design of the body is continued, to a lesser extent, in the Pointer some ten years later. *David Little*

GO-AHEAD NORTHERN

Go-Ahead Northern, 117 Queen Street, Bensham, Gateshead, Tyne & Wear, NE8 2UA

Subsidiaries, fleetnames and depots:
Gateshead & District Omnibus Co Ltd (Go-Ahead Gateshead): Stanley Road, Gateshead; Cromwell Place, Winlaton.
The Langley Park Motor Co Ltd (Gypsy Queen): Kingsway, Langley Park.
Low Fell Coaches Ltd (Low Fell): Lowreys Lane, Low Fell
The Northern General Transport Co Ltd (Northern): Picktree Lane, Chester-le-Street; Chester Road, Stanley; Leadgate Road, Consett.
The Northern National Omnibus Co (Voyager): Picktree Lane, Chester-le-Street
Sunderland & District Omnibus Co Ltd (Wear Buses): Philadelphia Lane, Philadelphia; Park Lane, Sunderland; Industrial Road, Washington
Tynemouth & District Omnibus Co Ltd (CoastLine): Hadrian Road, Wallsend; Norham Terrace, Percy Main.
Tyneside Omnibus Co Ltd (VFM Buses): Mile End Road, South Shields.
Venture Transport Co Ltd (Shaws): Callington Place, Craghead.
Visitauto Ltd (Metro Taxis): Norham Terrace, Percy Main, Mile End Road, South Shields

209-240				Mercedes-Benz L608D		Alexander AM		DP19F	1986-87		
209	C209PTY	216	C216PTY	222	C222PTY	228	D228URG	234	D234URG
210	C210PTY	217	C217PTY	223	C223PTY	229	D229URG	235	D235URG
211	C211PTY	218	C218PTY	224	C224PTY	230	D230URG	237	D237URG
212	C212PTY	219	C219PTY	225	D225URG	231	D231URG	238	D238URG
214	C214PTY	220	C220PTY	226	D226URG	232	D232URG	239	D239URG
215	C215PTY	221	C221PTY	227	D227URG	233	D233URG	240	D240URG

241	D241URG	Mercedes-Benz L608D	Reeve Burgess	DP19F	1987
242	D242URG	Mercedes-Benz L608D	Reeve Burgess	DP19F	1987

Following the take-over of Gypsy Queen, a number of Go-Ahead Northern vehicles have been transferred to that operation. The only mini-bus involved is 214 (C214PTY) a Mercedes-Benz L608D with Alexander AM bodywork. It is seen during May 1993 about to enter North Road, Durham. *Keith Grimes*

243-256

Renault-Dodge S56 — Alexander AM — DP19F* — 1987 — *243/5/50 are B19F

| 243 | D243VNL | 247 | D247VNL | 250 | D250VNL | 252 | D252VNL | 254 | D254VNL |
| 245 | D245VNL | 248 | D248VNL | 251 | D251VNL | 253 | D253VNL | 256 | D256VNL |

258-290

Renault-Dodge S56 — Alexander AM — DP19F* — 1986-87 *several now B19F

258	D258YBB	264	D264YBB	276	E276BRG	283	E283BRG	287	E287BRG
259	D259YBB	265	D265YBB	279	E279BRG	284	E284BRG	288	E288BRG
260	D260YBB	271	E271BRG	280	E280BRG	285	E285BRG	289	E289BRG
261	D261YBB	273	E273BRG	281	E281BRG	286	E286BRG	290	E290BRG
263	D263YBB	274	E274BRG	282	E282BRG				

291-310

Renault-Dodge S56 — Alexander AM — B25F — 1987-88 291 ex Alexander demo, 1988

291	E38OMS	295	E295ETY	299	E899GCU	303	E903GCU	307	E907GCU
292	E292ETY	296	E296ETY	300	E900GCU	304	E904GCU	308	E908GCU
293	E293ETY	297	E297ETY	301	E901GCU	305	E905GCU	309	E909GCU
294	E294ETY	298	E898GCU	302	E902GCU	306	E906GCU	310	E910GCU

311-316

Iveco Daily 49.10 — Reeve Burgess Beaver — B25F — 1989

| 311 | F311MTN | 313 | F313MTN | 314 | F314MTN | 315 | F315MTN | 316 | F316MTN |
| 312 | F312MTN | | | | | | | | |

317	E291VOM	Iveco Daily 49.10	Carlyle Dailybus 2	B25F	1988	Ex London Buses, 1989
318	E292VOM	Iveco Daily 49.10	Carlyle Dailybus 2	B25F	1988	Ex London Buses, 1989
319	E293VOM	Iveco Daily 49.10	Carlyle Dailybus 2	B25F	1988	Ex London Buses, 1989
320	E294VOM	Iveco Daily 49.10	Carlyle Dailybus 2	B25F	1988	Ex London Buses, 1989
321	C172WVT	Ford Transit 190D	Robin Hood	B16F	1986	
322	C173WVT	Ford Transit 190D	Robin Hood	B16F	1986	
330	C428AHT	Ford Transit 190D	Carlyle	B16F	1986	Ex Bristol, 1989
331	FGD847X	Mercedes-Benz L508D	Devon	B19F	1982	Ex Visitauto, 1989
332	A854TDS	Mercedes-Benz L608D	Reeve Burgess	C19F	1983	Ex Bain, Kemnay, 1989

333-346

Optare MetroRider MR03 — Optare — B26F — 1991

333	J933JJR	336	J936JJR	339	J939JJR	342	J942JJR	345	J945JJR
334	J934JJR	337	J937JJR	340	J940JJR	343	J943JJR	346	J946JJR
335	J935JJR	338	J938JJR	341	J941JJR	344	J944JJR		

348	A708GPR	Mercedes-Benz L608D	Reeve Burgess	C19F	1984	Ex Shaws, Craghead, 1992
349	C27LTN	Talbot Express	Steedrive	C14F	1985	Ex Shaws, Craghead, 1992

351-367

Optare MetroRider MR03 — Optare — B26F — 1993

351	K351SCN	355	K355SCN	359	K359SCN	362	K362SCN	365	K365SCN
352	K352SCN	356	K356SCN	360	K360SCN	363	K363SCN	366	K366SCN
353	K353SCN	357	K357SCN	361	K361SCN	364	K364SCN	367	K367SCN
354	K354SCN	358	K358SCN						

Most of the 14 Optare Metroriders delivered in 1991 wear a special Metro Centre Mini livery for the services to the shopping centre. No.342 (J942JJR) is seen about to enter the Metro Centre bus station on service M1. *Steve Warburton*

368	E522DCU	Mercedes-Benz L307D	Devon Conversions	M12	1987	Ex Low Fell Coaches, 1992
369	F901JBB	Mercedes-Benz 609D	Reeve Burgess	B25F	1988	Ex Low Fell Coaches, 1992
370	G703NGR	Mercedes-Benz 709D	Reeve Burgess Beaver	B25F	1990	Ex Low Fell Coaches, 1992
371	J829HTN	Mercedes-Benz 814D	Whittaker	C33F	1991	Ex Low Fell Coaches, 1992

372-377

Optare MetroRider MR03 — Optare — B26F — 1993

372	L972MTY	374	L974MTY	375	L975MTY	376	L976MTY	377	L977MTY
373	L973MTY								

2099	EDS508B	AEC Routemaster 3R2RH	Park Royal	H41/31F	1964	On extended loan
3285	RCN111N	Leyland Atlantean AN68/1R	Park Royal	O43/34F	1974	Ex Gateshead & District, 1976

3401-3444

Bristol VRT/SL3/501 — Eastern Coach Works — H43/31F — 1979

3401	JPT901T	3425	JPT925T	3430	JPT930T	3434	JPT934T	3442	SGR942V
3409	JPT909T	3426	JPT926T	3431	JPT931T	3435	SGR935V	3443	SGR943V
3413	JPT913T	3427	JPT927T	3433	JPT933T	3440	SGR940V	3444	SGR944V
3424	JPT924T								

3446-3485

Leyland Atlantean AN68B/1R — Roe — H43/30F — 1980

3446	AUP346W	3454	AUP354W	3462	AUP362W	3470	AUP370W	3478	AUP378W
3447	AUP347W	3455	AUP355W	3463	AUP363W	3471	AUP371W	3479	AUP379W
3448	AUP348W	3456	AUP356W	3464	AUP364W	3472	AUP372W	3480	AUP380W
3449	AUP349W	3457	AUP357W	3465	AUP365W	3473	AUP373W	3481	AUP381W
3450	AUP350W	3458	AUP358W	3466	AUP366W	3474	AUP374W	3482	AUP382W
3451	AUP351W	3459	AUP359W	3467	AUP367W	3475	AUP375W	3483	AUP383W
3452	AUP352W	3460	AUP360W	3468	AUP368W	3476	AUP376W	3484	AUP384W
3453	AUP353W	3461	AUP361W	3469	AUP369W	3477	AUP377W	3485	AUP385W

3486-3500

MCW Metrobus DR101/11 — MCW — H46/30F — 1980

3486	DVK486W	3489	DVK489W	3492	DVK492W	3495	DVK495W	3498	DVK498W
3487	DVK487W	3490	DVK490W	3493	DVK493W	3496	DVK496W	3499	DVK499W
3488	DVK488W	3491	DVK491W	3494	DVK494W	3497	DVK497W	3500	DVK500W

Now part of the Metro Taxis fleet, Leyland Atlantean/Park Royal open-topper 3285 (RCN111N) is seen at Whitley Bay Caravan Park on a blustery day in June 1993. *Bill Potter*

3501-3510 — MCW Metrobus DR102/37* — MCW — H46/31F — 1983 — *3506-10 are DR132/1

3501	UTN501Y	**3503**	UTN503Y	**3505**	UTN505Y	**3507**	UTN507Y	**3509**	UTN509Y
3502	UTN502Y	**3504**	UTN504Y	**3506**	UTN506Y	**3508**	UTN508Y	**3510**	UTN510Y

3520	C520LJR	Leyland Olympian ONCL10/1RV	Eastern Coach Works	DPH45/27F 1985
3521	C521LJR	Leyland Olympian ONCL10/1RV	Eastern Coach Works	DPH45/27F 1985
3522	C522LJR	Leyland Olympian ONCL10/1RV	Eastern Coach Works	DPH45/27F 1985
3523	C523LJR	Leyland Olympian ONCL10/1RV	Eastern Coach Works	DPH45/27F 1985

3524-3533 — Leyland Atlantean AN68A/2R — Alexander AL — DPH45/33F 1981 — Ex Tyne & Wear PTE, 1981

3524	EJR124W	**3526**	EJR126W	**3528**	EJR128W	**3530**	EJR130W	**3532**	EJR132W
3525	EJR125W	**3527**	EJR127W	**3529**	EJR129W	**3531**	EJR131W	**3533**	EJR133W

3535-3571 — Leyland Atlantean AN68A/1R — Eastern Coach Works — H43/31F — 1979-80

3535	MBR435T	**3543**	MBR443T	**3550**	MBR450T	**3557**	MBR457T	**3564**	SGR964V
3536	MBR436T	**3544**	MBR444T	**3551**	MBR451T	**3558**	MBR458T	**3566**	SUP266V
3537	MBR437T	**3545**	MBR445T	**3552**	MBR452T	**3559**	MBR459T	**3567**	SUP267V
3538	MBR438T	**3546**	MBR446T	**3553**	MBR453T	**3560**	MBR460T	**3568**	SUP268V
3539	MBR439T	**3547**	MBR447T	**3554**	MBR454T	**3561**	MBR461T	**3569**	SUP269V
3540	MBR440T	**3548**	MBR448T	**3555**	MBR455T	**3562**	MBR462T	**3570**	SUP270V
3541	MBR441T	**3549**	MBR449T	**3556**	MBR456T	**3563**	MBR463T	**3571**	SUP271V
3542	MBR442T								

3572-3617 — Leyland Olympian ONLXB/1R — Eastern Coach Works — H45/32F — 1981-83

3572	JTY372X	**3582**	JTY382X	**3591**	JTY391X	**3600**	JTY400X	**3609**	JTY369X
3573	JTY373X	**3583**	JTY383X	**3592**	JTY392X	**3601**	JTY401X	**3610**	JTY370X
3574	JTY374X	**3584**	JTY384X	**3593**	JTY393X	**3602**	JTY402X	**3611**	JTY371X
3575	JTY375X	**3585**	JTY385X	**3594**	JTY394X	**3603**	JTY403X	**3612**	SJR612Y
3576	JTY376X	**3586**	JTY386X	**3595**	JTY395X	**3604**	JTY404X	**3613**	SJR613Y
3577	JTY377X	**3587**	JTY387X	**3596**	JTY396X	**3605**	JTY405X	**3614**	SJR614Y
3578	JTY378X	**3588**	JTY388X	**3597**	JTY397X	**3606**	JTY406X	**3615**	SJR615Y
3579	JTY379X	**3589**	JTY389X	**3598**	JTY398X	**3607**	JTY407X	**3616**	SJR616Y
3580	JTY380X	**3590**	JTY390X	**3599**	JTY399X	**3608**	JTY368X	**3617**	SJR617Y
3581	JTY381X								

Opposite, Top: **'Northern - proud of our routes'** is prominent on the livery used by Go-Ahead Northern vehicles based at Chester-le-Street, Stanley and Consett. A Dennis Dart, with bodywork by Wright of Ballymena, 6039 (J639KCU) is seen arriving in Durham. *Keith Grimes*

Opposite, Bottom: **Optare, a member of the United Bus Group, has taken over the production of the MetroRider** originally built by MCW. Now constructed in integral form at Optare's Leeds site, it is becoming a popular vehicle around the country with total production reaching 1500. Part of an order for seventeen built in 1993, 359 (K359SCN) is seen in the new livery of Go-Ahead Gateshead. *Michael Fowler*

The Tyneside Omnibus operation of Go-Ahead is based at South Shields and has adopted the VFM Buses identity, using a two-tone blue livery, at the beginning of 1992. Roe-bodied Leyland Atlantean 3463 (AUP363W) is seen at Kepple Street, South Shields. *Keith Grimes*

The vehicles allocated to Percy Main garage carry a red and cream livery and the Go-Ahead Northern fleetname is now only carried by vehicles waiting for a repaint. Eastern Coach Works-bodied Leyland Atlantean, 3540 (MBR440T), is seen about to depart on service 305 to Newcastle. *Bill Potter*

A few vehicles operating out of Sunderland and Philadelphia depots still carry the red and white livery with small Wear Buses transfers. Former Tyne and Wear PTE Leyland Atlantean with an MCW body, 3715 (YNL215V) is entering Park Lane bus station, Sunderland. *Bill Potter*

Tynemouth and District now operate as CoastLine in a red and cream livery similar to that used by the old Tynemouth company. No.3600 (JTY400X) is seen at Whitley Bay Bandstand operating service 317 to North Shields Ferry. *Bill Potter*

All five Alexander-bodied Leyland Olympians are allocated to Go-Ahead Gateshead's Winlaton depot. Leaving Newgate Street, Newcastle on one of the group of services to the Winlaton area is 3678 (G678TCN). *Steve Warburton*

The remaining Bristol VRTs have standard NBC-supplied Eastern Coach Works bodies and operate out of Northern's Chester-le-Street depot. No.3427 (JPT927T) is seen at Washington Galleries bus station on service 551 to South Shields. The new style fleetname is displayed on the side of the vehicle.
Steve Warburton

The link road between the Tyne Bridge and the road from the High Level Bridge is the setting for 3628 (A628BCN), operating service 231 to Hartlepool. The pub to the right of the bus is one of the smallest on Tyneside.
Steve Warburton

The fifteen original Mark 1 MCW Metrobuses are all allocated to Go-Ahead Gateshead. Approaching Gateshead Metro Interchange is 3497 (DVK497W) illustrating the type in the new livery.
Bill Potter

3618-3648

MCW Metrobus DR102/43 MCW H46/31F 1984

3618	A618BCN	3625	A625BCN	3631	A631BCN	3637	A637BCN	3643	A643BCN
3619	A619BCN	3626	A626BCN	3632	A632BCN	3638	A638BCN	3644	A644BCN
3620	A620BCN	3627	A627BCN	3633	A633BCN	3639	A639BCN	3645	A645BCN
3621	A621BCN	3628	A628BCN	3634	A634BCN	3640	A640BCN	3646	A646BCN
3622	A622BCN	3629	A629BCN	3635	A635BCN	3641	A641BCN	3647	A647BCN
3623	A623BCN	3630	A630BCN	3636	A636BCN	3642	A642BCN	3648	A648BCN
3624	A624BCN								

3649-3674

Leyland Olympian ONCL10/1RV* Eastern Coach Works H45/32F* 1985 *3652/63/7-71 are DPH40/30F
*3674 has a Gardner 5HLXCT engine

3649	C649LJR	3655	C655LJR	3660	C660LJR	3665	C665LJR	3670	C670LJR
3650	C650LJR	3656	C656LJR	3661	C661LJR	3666	C666LJR	3671	C671LJR
3651	C651LJR	3657	C657LJR	3662	C662LJR	3667	C667LJR	3672	C672LJR
3652	C652LJR	3658	C658LJR	3663	C663LJR	3668	C668LJR	3673	C673LJR
3653	C653LJR	3659	C659LJR	3664	C664LJR	3669	C669LJR	3674	C674LJR
3654	C654LJR								

3675-3679

Leyland Olympian ONCL10/1RZ Alexander RH H45/29F 1989

3675	G675TCN	3676	G676TCN	3677	G677TCN	3678	G678TCN	3679	G679TCN

3685-3703

Leyland Atlantean AN68/2R MCW H49/37F 1979 Ex Tyne & Wear PTE, 1982

3685	VFT185T	3692	VFT192T	3697	VFT197T	3701	VFT201T	3703	VFT203T
3691	VFT191T	3696	VFT196T	3700	VFT200T	3702	VFT202T		

3704-3733

Leyland Atlantean AN68A/2R MCW H49/37F 1979 Ex Tyne & Wear PTE, 1982

3704	YNL204V	3710	YNL210V	3717	YNL217V	3725	YNL225V	3730	YNL230V
3706	YNL206V	3711	YNL211V	3723	YNL223V	3726	YNL226V	3731	YNL231V
3707	YNL207V	3714	YNL214V	3724	YNL224V	3729	YNL229V	3733	YNL233V
3708	YNL208V	3715	YNL215V						

3734-3748

Leyland Olympian ONLC10/1RV Eastern Coach Works H45/32F 1985

3734	B734GCN	3737	B737GCN	3740	B740GCN	3743	B743GCN	3746	B746GCN
3735	B735GCN	3738	B738GCN	3741	B741GCN	3744	B744GCN	3747	B747GCN
3736	B736GCN	3739	B739GCN	3742	B742GCN	3745	B745GCN	3748	B748GCN

3749-3778

MCW Metrobus DR102/55 MCW H46/31F* 1986 *3756 is DPH43/29F

3749	C749OCN	3755	C755OCN	3761	C761OCN	3767	C767OCN	3773	C773OCN
3750	C750OCN	3756	C756OCN	3762	C762OCN	3768	C768OCN	3774	C774OCN
3751	C751OCN	3757	C757OCN	3763	C763OCN	3769	C769OCN	3775	C775OCN
3752	C752OCN	3758	C758OCN	3764	C764OCN	3770	C770OCN	3776	C776OCN
3753	C753OCN	3759	C759OCN	3765	C765OCN	3771	C771OCN	3777	C777OCN
3754	C754OCN	3760	C760OCN	3766	C766OCN	3772	C772OCN	3778	C778OCN

In 1986 Northern took delivery of 11 MCW Metrobuses for use on express work. Several of these, including 3787 (C787OCN), have received Wear Buses' two-tone green, grey and white livery modified slightly for Wear Express lettering. It is seen in Peterlee while operating service X5 to Newcastle.
Bill Potter

3779-3789

MCW Metrobus DR102/58   MCW   DPH43/29F 1986

3779	C779OCN	3782	C782OCN	3784	C784OCN	3786	C786OCN	3788	C788OCN
3780	C780OCN	3783	C783OCN	3785	C785OCN	3787	C787OCN	3789	C789OCN
3781	C781OCN								

4604	VPT604R	Leyland National 11351A/1R	B49F	1977
4605	XBR605R	Leyland National 11351A/1R	B49F	1977
4624	BPT904S	Leyland National 11351A/1R	B49F	1977
4634	KBR634T	Leyland National 11351A/1R	DP23DL	1978
4638	CPT638S	Leyland National 11351A/1R	B49F	1978
4652	MGR952T	Leyland National 11351A/1R	B49F	1979

4660-4685

Leyland National 2 NL116L11/1R   B49F*   1980   *4667 is B45F

4660	UPT660V	4665	UPT665V	4670	UPT670V	4675	UPT675V	4680	UPT680V
4661	UPT661V	4666	UPT666V	4671	UPT671V	4676	UPT676V	4681	UPT681V
4662	UPT662V	4667	UPT667V	4672	UPT672V	4677	UPT677V	4683	UPT683V
4663	UPT663V	4668	UPT668V	4673	UPT673V	4678	UPT678V	4684	UPT684V
4664	UPT664V	4669	UPT669V	4674	UPT674V	4679	UPT679V	4685	UPT685V

4686-4714

Leyland National 2 NL116L11/1R   B49F*   1980-81   *4698/700/12/4 are B45F

4686	BGR686W	4695	FTN695W	4701	FTN701W	4706	FTN706W	4711	FTN711W
4687	BGR687W	4697	FTN697W	4702	FTN702W	4707	FTN707W	4712	FTN712W
4688	BGR688W	4698	FTN698W	4703	FTN703W	4708	FTN708W	4713	FTN713W
4691	WPT691V	4699	FTN699W	4704	FTN704W	4709	FTN709W	4714	FTN714W
4694	FTN694W	4700	FTN700W	4705	FTN705W	4710	FTN710W		

4715-4721

Leyland National 2 NL116AHLXB/1R*   B49F   1983   *4717 is type NL116AHLXC/1R.

4715	TJR715Y	4717	TJR717Y	4719	TJR719Y	4720	TJR720Y	4721	TJR721Y
4716	TJR716Y	4718	TJR718Y						

4722-4733

Leyland Lynx LX1126LXCTZR1R* Leyland   B47F   1989
*4728/33 are type LX116TL11ZR1S; 4729-32 are LX1126LXCTZR1S; 4733 fitted with Cummins engine

4722	F722LRG	4725	F725LRG	4728	F728LRG	4730	F730LRG	4732	F732LRG
4723	F723LRG	4726	F726LRG	4729	F729LRG	4731	F731LRG	4733	F733LRG
4724	F724LRG	4727	F727LRG						

4734-4747

DAF SB220LC550   Optare Delta   B49F   1989

4734	G734RTY	4737	G737RTY	4740	G740RTY	4743	G743RTY	4746	G746RTY
4735	G735RTY	4738	G734 8TY	4741	G741RTY	4744	G744RTY	4747	G747RTY
4736	G736RTY	4739	G734 9TY	4742	G742RTY	4745	G745RTY		

4748	UUP830K	Leyland National 1151/1R/0402		B23DL	1972	Ex West Riding, 1989
4749	E107DJR	Volvo B10M-61	Duple 300	B55F	1987	Ex Gypsy Queen, Langley Park, 1989

4750-4754

DAF SB220LC550   Optare Delta   B49F   1990

4750	G755UCU	4751	G751UCU	4752	G752UCU	4753	G753UCU	4754	G754UCU

4755	H802OPT	Dennis Dart 9.8SDL3004	Carlyle Dartline	B40F	1991

4756-4761

DAF SB220LC550   Optare Delta   B49F   1993

4756	K756SBB	4758	K758SBB	4759	K759SBB	4760	K760SBB	4761	K761SBB
4757	K757SBB								

4762	B693JBB	Bedford YMT	Duple Laser 2	DP53F	1985	Ex Gypsy Queen, 1991
4763	C885MTN	Bedford YNT	Duple Dominant	DP49F	1985	Ex Low Fell Coaches, 1992
4764	D913URG	Bedford YMT	Plaxton Derwent II	DP49F	1987	Ex Low Fell Coaches, 1992
4765	D914URG	Bedford YMT	Plaxton Derwent II	B55F	1987	Ex Low Fell Coaches, 1992
4766	F902JBB	Leyland Tiger TRCTL11/3R	Duple 300	B55F	1988	Ex Low Fell Coaches, 1992
4767	H163DJU	Dennis Javelin 11SDL1914	Duple 300	B55F	1991	Ex Low Fell Coaches, 1992
4768	J110SPB	Dennis Lance 11SDA3101	Alexander PS	B51F	1992	Ex Dennis demonstrator, 1993

A few years ago a new unit, Venture Transport, was set up. This became operational at the beginning of August 1992 when Shaw of Craghead was acquired. Venture Transport now operates as Shaws Coaches in a blue and cream livery. Shaws Leyland National 2, 4700 (FTN700W) is seen in Worswick Street, Newcastle on a competing service to one operated by Classic of Annfield Plain. *Steve Warburton*

All the Leyland Lynx are allocated to the Sunderland and District unit. Their main sphere of operation is services 194 and 294 between Easington Lane or Harreston and Heworth which requires single deckers due to a low bridge on the route. The first of the batch, 4728 (F728LRG), is seen at Heworth in June 1993 and illustrates the route branding on the Wear Buses livery. *Phillip Stephenson*

The first Dennis Dart for the Go-Ahead fleet, and the only one bodied by Carlyle, was delivered to Gypsy Queen in May 1991. Numbered in the main series, 4755 (H802OPT) wears full Gypsy Queen livery and is seen leaving Durham for Langley Park. All of the Gypsy Queen vehicles have fleet numbers allocated, but these are not carried on the vehicles. *Steve Warburton*

The Visitauto operation was formed to operate minibuses for people visiting hospitals as out-patients. Following loss of this work, Tyne and Wear PTE tendered routes have been won for the unit. One such service is 33, from Heworth Metro to ASDA at Boldon Colliery. In Metro Taxis livery is 5110 (MPT710T) *Mike Fowler*

Although part of Go-Ahead Northern, Low Fell Coaches continue to operate separately. Like Gypsy Queen, fleet numbers are allocated but are not carried on the vehicles. Former demonstrator, 4768 (J110SPB) is a Dennis Lance with Alexander PS-type bodywork and is seen on the Cross Tyne Service in Pilgrim Street, Newcastle.
Steve Warburton

All but one of the K-registered Optare Deltas carry the special red, blue and yellow livery for Supershuttle, a service between Gateshead Metro Interchange and Metro Centre. Seen leaving the Interchange for the Metro Centre in this scheme is 4758 (K758SBB). *Steve Warburton*

The four Leyland Tigers allocated to VFM Buses are painted in a modified version of the two-tone blue livery with lettering for Two Cities Express. This is an express service between Sunderland and Newcastle and 5119 (A719ABB) is seen at the junction of Pilgrim Street and Market Street at the 'top' end of the route. *Steve Warburton*

Six Volvo B10M, with Plaxton Expressliner bodywork are operated by Northern National on National Express contracts. Two of these previously worked with Yorkshire Voyager and one of the pair, 7044 (H330UWT), is seen leaving Middlesbrough bus station on the final leg of its journey to Sunderland. *Steve Warburton*

5061	PPT761P	Leyland Leopard PSU3C/4RT	Plaxton Supreme III Express	C49F	1976
5070	EGR570S	Leyland Leopard PSU3E/4RT	Plaxton Supreme III Express	C49F	1978
5090	LFT90X	Leyland Leopard PSU3F/4R	Willowbrook 003	C49F	1981
5096	LFT96X	Leyland Leopard PSU3F/4R	Willowbrook 003	C49F	1981
5097	LFT97X	Leyland Leopard PSU3G/4R	Eastern Coach Works B51	C49F	1982
5099	LFT99X	Leyland Leopard PSU3G/4R	Eastern Coach Works B51	C49F	1982
5100	LFT100X	Leyland Leopard PSU3G/4R	Eastern Coach Works B51	C49F	1982

5101-5105   Leyland Tiger TRCTL11/3RH   Plaxton Paramount 3200 II   C51F   1986

5101	C101PCN	5102	C102PCN	5103	C103PCN	5104	C104PCN	5105	C105PCN

5106	EGR706S	Leyland Leopard PSU3E/4RT	Plaxton Supreme III Express	C49F	1978	
5110	MPT710T	Leyland Leopard PSU3E/4RT	Plaxton Supreme IV	C49F	1979	
5111	HCU11W	Leyland Leopard PSU3G/4R	Duple Dominant IV	C49F	1980	
5113	C537OTY	Bedford YMP	Plaxton Paramount 3200	DP45F	1986	Ex Gypsy Queen, Langley Park, 1989
5114	C538OTY	Bedford YMP	Duple Laser 2	DP45F	1986	Ex Gypsy Queen, Langley Park, 1989

5116-5120   Leyland Tiger TRCTL11/2R   Plaxton Paramount 3200 E   C44FT   1984

5116	A716ABB	5117	A717ABB	5118	A718ABB	5119	A719ABB	5120	A720ABB

5121	UWA99S	Leyland Leopard PSU3E/4R	Duple Dominant II	C46F	1977	Ex Shaw, Craghead, 1992
5122	DBB32V	Leyland Leopard PSU3E/4R	Plaxton Supreme IV	C48FT	1980	Ex Shaw, Craghead, 1992
5123	LOA833X	Leyland Leopard PSU3F/4R	Willowbrook 003	C49F	1982	Ex Low Fell Coaches, 1992
5125	JSK254	Leyland Tiger TRCTL11/3RH	Plaxton Paramount 3200	C50F	1985	
5126	GSK962	Leyland Tiger TRCTL11/3RH	Plaxton Paramount 3200	C50F	1985	
7012	PCN762	Leyland Royal Tiger B50	Roe Doyen	C44FT	1983	
7024	574CPT	Leyland Tiger TRCTL11/3RH	Plaxton Paramount 3500 II	C48FT	1985	
7027	JSK327	Leyland Tiger TRCTL11/3R	Plaxton Paramount 3200 IIE	C46FT	1985	
7028	JSK328	Leyland Tiger TRCTL11/3R	Plaxton Paramount 3200 IIE	C46FT	1985	
7031	E131CTN	Leyland Tiger TRCTL11/3RZ	Plaxton Paramount 3500 III	C46FT	1988	
7032	CU6860	Leyland Tiger TRCTL11/3ARZ	Plaxton Paramount 3500 III	C51FT	1989	
7033	CU7661	Leyland Tiger TRCTL11/3ARZ	Plaxton Paramount 3500 III	C51FT	1989	
7034	961KVK	DAF MB230	Duple 340	C53F	1986	Ex Happy Days, Woodseaves, 1989
7035	340GUP	DAF MB230	Duple 340	C53F	1986	Ex Happy Days, Woodseaves, 1989
7037	E102DJR	Volvo B10M-46	Plaxton Paramount 3200 III	C43F	1988	Ex Gypsy Queen, Langley Park, 1989
7038	JCN822	Leyland Tiger TRCTL11/3RZ	Plaxton Paramount 3500 III	C51FT	1988	Ex Fishwick, Leyland, 1990
7039	H139CVK	Volvo B10M-60	Plaxton Expressliner	C49FT	1990	
7040	H140CVK	Volvo B10M-60	Plaxton Expressliner	C49FT	1990	
7041	H141CVK	Volvo B10M-60	Plaxton Expressliner	C49FT	1990	
7042	H142CVK	Volvo B10M-60	Plaxton Expressliner	C49FT	1990	
7043	H329UWT	Volvo B10M-60	Plaxton Expressliner	C49FT	1990	Ex Yorkshire Voyager, 1991
7044	H330UWT	Volvo B10M-60	Plaxton Expressliner	C49FT	1990	Ex Yorkshire Voyager, 1991
7045	425BVK	Leyland Tiger TRCL10/3ARZM	Plaxton Paramount 3500 III	C49FT	1989	Ex Plymouth, 1991
7046	JSK346	Volvo B10M-60	Plaxton Paramount 3500 III	C53FT	1990	Ex Hill's, Tredegar, 1992

Three Willowbrook-bodied Leyland Leopards remain in service with the Go-Ahead group, two were new to Northern while the third originated with Midland Red. Now painted into Metro Taxis livery is 5096 (LFT96X), one of the original pair, seen heading for the Asda superstore at Boldon.
Steve Warburton

67

The establishment of the VFM Buses identity on South Tyneside coincided with the delivery of 13 Dennis Darts. All are fitted with Wright's Handy-bus body and 8007 (J607KCU) is seen between duties at Heworth Metro. *Steve Warburton*

The delivery of ten Dennis Darts to Sunderland and District at the beginning of September 1992 saw the introduction of the two-tone green, grey and white livery for the Wear Buses identity. One of the batch, 8064 (K864PCN), is seen at Heworth Metro operating service 130, the more direct of two routes from there to Sunderland. *Mike Fowler*

7047	524FUP	Leyland Tiger TRCTL11/3ARZ	Plaxton Paramount 3500 III	C55FT	1989	Ex Fishwick, Leyland, 1992
7048	F597BTG	Leyland Tiger TRCL10/3ARZM	Plaxton Paramount 3500 III	C51FT	1989	Ex Hill's, Tredegar, 1992
7049	FCU190	Leyland Tiger TRCL10/3ARZM	Plaxton Paramount 3500 III	C51FT	1989	Ex Anslow, Garndiffaith, 1992
7050	EIB1647	Leyland Tiger TRCTL11/3R	Plaxton Paramount 3500	C49FT	1983	Ex Shaws, Craghead, 1992
7051	EIB8955	Leyland Tiger TRCTL11/3R	Plaxton Paramount 3500	C49FT	1983	Ex Shaws, Craghead, 1992
7052	K2VOY	Volvo B10M-60	Plaxton Expressliner II	C46FT	1993	
7053	K3VOY	Volvo B10M-60	Plaxton Expressliner II	C46FT	1993	
7054	E151AGG	Dennis Javelin 11SDA1906	Plaxton Paramount 3200 III	C51F	1988	Ex Southern, Barrhead, 1993
7055	E980KJF	Dennis Javelin 11SDL1905	Duple 320	C53F	1988	Ex Torr, Gedling, 1992

8001-8040

Dennis Dart 9.8SDL3017 — Wright Handy-bus — B40F — 1991

8001	J601KCU	8009	J609KCU	8017	J617KCU	8025	J625KCU	8033	J633KCU
8002	J602KCU	8010	J610KCU	8018	J618KCU	8026	J626KCU	8034	J634KCU
8003	J603KCU	8011	J611KCU	8019	J619KCU	8027	J627KCU	8035	J635KCU
8004	J604KCU	8012	J612KCU	8020	J620KCU	8028	J628KCU	8036	J636KCU
8005	J605KCU	8013	J613KCU	8021	J621KCU	8029	J629KCU	8037	J637KCU
8006	J606KCU	8014	J614KCU	8022	J622KCU	8030	J630KCU	8038	J638KCU
8007	J607KCU	8015	J615KCU	8023	J623KCU	8031	J631KCU	8039	J639KCU
8008	J608KCU	8016	J616KCU	8024	J624KCU	8032	J632KCU	8040	J640KCU

8041-8065

Dennis Dart 9.8SDL3017 — Wright Handy-bus — B40F — 1992

8041	J941MFT	8046	J946MFT	8051	J951MFT	8056	K856PCN	8061	K861PCN
8042	J942MFT	8047	J947MFT	8052	J952MFT	8057	K857PCN	8062	K862PCN
8043	J943MFT	8048	J948MFT	8053	J953MFT	8058	K858PCN	8063	K863PCN
8044	J944MFT	8049	J949MFT	8054	J954MFT	8059	K859PCN	8064	K864PCN
8045	J945MFT	8050	J950MFT	8055	J955MFT	8060	K860PCN	8065	K865PCN

8066-8089

Dennis Dart 9.8SDL3017 — Wright Handy-bus — B40F — 1993

8066	K366RTY	8071	K371RTY	8076	K376RTY	8081	K381RTY	8086	K986SCU
8067	K367RTY	8072	K372RTY	8077	K377RTY	8082	K382RTY	8087	K987SCU
8068	K368RTY	8073	K373RTY	8078	K378RTY	8083	K383RTY	8088	K988SCU
8069	K369RTY	8074	K374RTY	8079	K379RTY	8084	K984SCU	8089	K989SCU
8070	K370RTY	8075	K375RTY	8080	K380RTY	8085	K985SCU		

Operators and Liveries:

Go-Ahead Gateshead (Red, white and blue): 250/6/71/3/9, 302/3/6-9/33-46/51-67, 3486-99, 3500/74/84/7/94, 3618/25-7/9-31/3-9/42-6/54-6/75-9, 3734-41/9-54/60-6/9-74/8, 4664/6/7, 4750-61, 8016-25/66-83.

Gypsy Queen (Cream, red and blue): 214, 4749, 5112-4, 7036/7

Northern (Cream and red): 219/21-3/6-31/8, 304/5/10/7/9/20, 3401/9/13/24-7/30/1/3-5/40/2-4, 3506-10/20-3/35/41/2/4/6/9/51/9/66/8-70/83/96, 3620/1/3/4/8/32/41/7/57-9/75/9/80/5/8, 4660/1/8-70/6/8, 4702/18/9/21/34-47, 5102-5.

Voyager (Red and gold, or National Express): 4634, 7024/7/8/31-5/8-49/52/3.

Low Fell Coaches (White and blue): 368-71, 4657, 4762-68, 5114, 7054/5

Shaws (Cream and blue): 232/41/2, 348/9, 4604/5/24/38, 4700/13/4, 5090, 5106.21-3, 7050/1.

Wear Buses (Green, grey and white): 209-12/5-18/24/5/33-5/7/9/40/7/8//53/4/63-5/74/80-97, 311-6, 3450/6/71/6/9, 3501-5/82/6/91/5/7/9, 3604/10/1/3/5/6/9/22/40/8/51/2/7/9-81/3-6/8/91/4/5/7-9, 4701/3-12/5-7/20/2-33, 5061/97/9, 5100/1/11/8, 8056-65.

Coastline (Cream and red): 243/5/51/5/8-61/76/98-301, 2099, 3600/1-3/5-9/14/53/8/69/70/1/4, 3743-48, 8014/5/84-9.

VFM Buses (Two-tone blue and grey): 3451/8-61/9/73/7/80, 3524-33/8-40/53-4/7/72/3/7/-81/5/92/3/3600, 3704/7/8, 4662/72/87, 5116-20, 8001-13

Metro Taxis (Yellow, black and white): 220, 321/2/30/2, 3285, 3536/7/52/67, 4634, 5070/96, 5110.

Previous Registrations:

340GUP	C776MVH	DBB32V	MNM32V, 369FKF	JCN822	E116KFV
425BVK	G349RTA	EDS508B	RCN699	JSK254	B25HTY
524FUP	F57YCW	EIB1647	BFP4Y	JSK327	C27LJR
574CPT	B24GVK	EIB8955	JBT835Y	JSK328	C28LJR
961KVK	C774MVH	FCU190	F596BTG	JSK346	G61RGG
CU6860	F32LCU	GSK962	B26HTY	GSK962	B26HTY
CU7661	F33LCU	PCN762	A212XJR		

GREENCROFT COACHES

B & V M Walker, Ashlea, Greencroft Road, New Greencroft, Co Durham, DH9 8PF

Depot: North Road Garage, Catchgate

LRG446X	Mercedes-Benz L207D	Devon Conversions	M12	1982	Ex Craiggs, Radcliffe, 1991
C555XVU	Mercedes-Benz L207D	Charterway Cocker	M12	1986	
C807CBU	Renault-Dodge S56	Northern Counties	B22F	1986	Ex GM Buses, 1991
C812CBU	Renault-Dodge S56	Northern Counties	B22F	1986	Ex GM Buses, 1991
C902FMP	Bedford CFL	Dormobile	M16	1986	Ex Victoria Shuttle, London, 1990
D760MUR	Iveco Daily 49.10	Robin Hood City Nippy	B21F	1986	Ex Luton & District, 1989
BW3113	Mercedes-Benz 609D	Reeve Burgess	B20F	1987	Ex Low Fell Coaches, 1991
D453OPP	Ford Transit	Chassis Developments	M16	1987	Ex Chatfield, Worthing, 1991
D919KDB	Mercedes-Benz L307D	Walker		1987	
E488VHL	Mercedes-Benz L207D	Walker	M5L	1988	
F233NVK	Ford Transit VE6	Walker	M14	1989	Ex Cowie Leasing, Sunderland, 1993

Livery: Green and silver-grey

Previous Registrations:
BW3113   D915URG

Greencroft Coaches operate a varied selection of mini and midi buses. Former Luton & District D760MUR, an Iveco Daily with Robin Hood City Nippy bodywork, was operating a school journey in Lanchester during the summer of 1993. *David Little*

GRIERSON

D & C J Grierson, Sedgefield Road Garage, Fishburn, Co Durham, TS21 4DD

847LAA	Volvo B58-56	Plaxton Elite III Express	C53F	1974	Ex Hills, Stibb Cross, 1990
ARF149S	Volvo B58-61	Plaxton Supreme III	C53F	1978	Ex Baker, Biddulph, 1991
668HCG	Volvo B58-61	Plaxton Supreme III	C51F	1978	Ex Fairley, Spennymoor, 1989
GVL323	Volvo B58-61	Plaxton Supreme IV	C53F	1979	Ex Harry Shaw, Coventry, 1982
MHP2V	Ford R1114	Plaxton Supreme IV	C49F	1980	Ex Red House, Coventry, 1982
LIB987	Volvo B58-61	Plaxton Viewmaster IV	C40FT	1981	Ex Elite, Stockport, 1991
KJR279X	Mercedes-Benz L207D	Whittaker	M12	1981	Ex Masters & Milburn, 1983
SBB85Y	Mercedes-Benz L508D	Reeve Burgess	DP19F	1982	Ex National Blood Transfusion ,1992
TXI8757	Volvo B10M-61	Jonckheere Jubilee P90	CH49/9FT	1983	Ex Pat's, New Broughton, 1992
LIB347	Volvo B10M-61	Jonckheere Jubilee P90	CH34/9FT	1983	Ex A-one, Heywood, 1991
LIB854	Volvo B10M-61	Plaxton Paramount 3500	C53FT	1984	Ex Stonehouse, Brotton, 1988
1725LJ	Volvo B10M-61	Plaxton Paramount 3500	C49F	1984	Ex Jack, Dunfermline, 1985
LIB447	Volvo B10M-61	Jonckheere Jubilee P50	CH47/10FT	1984	Ex Guards, Purfleet, 1987
B417CGG	Volvo B10M-53	Van Hool Astral	CH50/12FT	1985	Ex ??, 1993
LIB449	Volvo B10M-53	Jonckheere Jubilee P95	CH52/13FT	1986	
E920KBF	Ford Transit VE6	Dormobile	M16	1986	Ex Viking, Heywood, 1993
E126RAX	Freight Rover Sherpa 410	Carlyle Citybus 2	B20F	1987	Ex Cynon Valley, 1992
E435YSU	Mercedes-Benz 609D	Scott	C25F	1988	
H424DVM	Mercedes-Benz 609D	Made-to-Measure	C24F	1990	Ex Varteg, Garndiffaith, 1991
G462BAY	Leyland-DAF 400	Crystals	M16	1990	Ex Hayes, Frampton West, 1991
G262GKG	Freight Rover Sherpa 410	Carlyle Citybus 2	B20F	1990	Ex National Welsh, 1992
G930MAO	Volvo B10M-61	Plaxton Paramount 3500 III	C51FT	1990	Ex Gordon, Kirkbride, 1991
G151UAS	Leyland-DAF 400	Dormobile	B20F	1990	Ex Inverness Traction, 1990

Livery: Red and white (buses); white and blue (coaches).

Previous Registrations:

1725LJ	A797TGG	LIB447	B513CBD
668HCG	XWX201S	LIB449	C415LRP
847LAA	PUT313M, 138ASV	LIB854	A620UGD
ARF149S	XEH2S, 5658RU	LIB987	SLH8W, 6242BY
GVL323	HVC16V	TXI8757	MRP837Y, GSV957, LHO942Y
LIB347	BFP1Y		

Many coaches in the Grierson fleet carry cherished registrations. This Volvo B10M with a mark 1 Paramount body is no exception. Originally registered A797TGG it now carries 1725LJ and is seen with this mark is it passes through Harrogate .
Colin Lloyd

HARTLEPOOL TRANSPORT

Hartlepool Transport Ltd, 1 Church Street, Hartlepool, Cleveland, TS24 7DS

1-7

| | | | | | | | Leyland National 11351A/2R | | | B46D* | 1977 | *2 is B49F, 7 is B50F |

1	SHN401R	3	SHN403R	5	SHN405R	6	SHN406R	7	SHN407R
2	SHN402R	4	SHN404R

(Row 1): 1 SHN401R, 3 SHN403R, 5 SHN405R, 6 SHN406R, 7 SHN407R
(Row 2): 2 SHN402R, 4 SHN404R

14-20

Leyland National 2 NL116L11/2R — B46D* — 1980 — *15/16 are DP47F, 18 DP50F, 19 B50F

| 14 | KAJ214W | 16 | KAJ216W | 18 | KAJ218W | 19 | KAJ219W | 20 | KAJ220W |
| 15 | KAJ215W | 17 | KAJ217W |

21-26

Dennis Falcon HC SDA409 — Wadham Stringer — B46D — 1983

| 21 | YDC21Y | 23 | YDC23Y | 24 | YDC24Y | 25 | YDC25Y | 26 | YDC26Y |
| 22 | YDC22Y |

27-32

Dennis Falcon HC SDA409 — Northern Counties — B47D — 1985

| 27 | B27PAJ | 29 | B29PAJ | 30 | B30PAJ | 31 | B31PAJ | 32 | B32PAJ |
| 28 | B28PAJ |

38	RUF38R	Leyland National 11351A/2R	B44D	1977	Ex Brighton & Hove, 1990
40	RUF40R	Leyland National 11351A/2R	B44D	1977	Ex Brighton & Hove, 1990
49	UFG49S	Leyland National 11351A/2R	B44D	1977	Ex Brighton & Hove, 1990
52	UFG52S	Leyland National 11351A/2R	B50F	1977	Ex Brighton & Hove, 1990

59-79

Bristol RELL6L — Eastern Coach Works — B46D — 1970-72

59	LEF59H	65	MEF65J	70	MEF70J	74	OEF74K	77	OEF77K
60	LEF60H	66	MEF66J	71	MEF71J	75	OEF75K	78	OEF78K
61	LEF61H	67	MEF67J	72	MEF72J	76	OEF76K	79	OEF79K
64	LEF64H	69	MEF69J	73	OEF73K

80-96

Bristol RELL6L — Eastern Coach Works — B46D* — 1973-75 — *91 is DP47F

80	SEF80L	84	SEF84L	88	GEF188N	91	GEF191N	94	JAJ294N
81	SEF81L	85	GEF185N	89	GEF189N	92	JAJ292N	95	JAJ295N
82	SEF82L	86	GEF186N	90	GEF190N	93	JAJ293N	96	JAJ296N
83	SEF83L	87	GEF187N

101	XCC94V	Leyland Leopard PSU3E/4R	Plaxton Supreme IV Express C49F	1980	Ex Vale of Llangollen, 1986
102	BTU33W	Leyland Leopard PSU3E/4R	Plaxton Supreme IV Express C49F	1981	Ex Vale of Llangollen, 1986
103	FSL61W	Leyland Leopard PSU3G/4R	Plaxton Supreme IV Express C49F	1982	Ex Tayside, 1987
104	FSL62W	Leyland Leopard PSU3G/4R	Plaxton Supreme IV Express C49F	1982	Ex Tayside, 1987
105	HDZ8683	Volvo B10M-61	Plaxton Paramount 3500 C49F	1984	Ex Allander, Milngavie, 1989
106	837XHW	Leyland Leopard PSU3/4R	Plaxton Supreme IV(1979) C41F	1965	Ex Matthews, Cwmbran, 1990

Livery: Ivory and maroon
Overall adverstisment: 7, 14/7/8, 78.

Previous Registrations:

837XHW	CHA106C, WHT825T	FSL62W	ESL306W, 6689DP
BTU33W	WLG380W, 93FYB	HDZ8683	A845UGB, 2367AT, A491WYS
FSL61W	ESL307W, 666TPJ	XCC94V	UMA953V, UAM829

Four Leyland Nationals formerly with Brighton and Hove are operated by Hartlepool. Three are dual-door examples while 52 (UFG52S) is now converted to single door. It is seen in Hartlepool, working a Cleveland County Council tendered service to Greatham. *Bill Potter*

Bristol RE 77 (OEF77K), with Eastern Coach Works body is now over 20-years old, and is seen on service 7 to Middlegate. Middlegate was situated in the old borough of Hartlepool which combined with its larger neighbour, West Hartlepool, in 1967 the enlarged borough being known simply as Hartlepool. *Bill Potter*

Hartlepool operate a small coach fleet with all but one vehicle being Leyland Leopards. One example, with a Plaxton Supreme body, is 104 (FSL62W) which carried ESL306W when new. Seen passing through Haymarket bus station in Newcastle while heading for the Metro Centre it shows it is an express doorway variant. *Keith Grimes*

Hartlepool's last batch of Bristol REs were delivered as long ago as 1975. Displaying its dual doorway, and devoid of any opening windows, 94 (JAJ294N) was photographed in Hartlepool town centre while working service 7 to Middlegate. *Bill Potter*

Having standardised on the Bristol RE/Eastern Coach Works combination for many years, the next type supplied to Hartlepool was the Dennis Falcon HC. Two batches have been taken into stock, each having a different body manufacturer. One of the second batch, with Northern Counties bodies, is 27 (B27PAJ), seen in Victoria Road during May 1993. *Keith Grimes*

HENNINGS

D Henning, 17 Station Road West, Trimdon Station, Co Durham.

XHS116S	Ford R1114	Plaxton Supreme III	C53F	1977	Ex Collingwood, Wheatley Hill, 1992
DBA81T	Ford R1114	Plaxton Supreme III	C53F	1978	Ex Collingwood, Wheatley Hill, 1992
CFX325T	Ford R1114	Plaxton Supreme IV	C49F	1979	Ex Blessed, Bolton-on-Dearne, 1992
XGB63W	Volvo B58-61	Duple Dominant III	C50F	1981	Ex Stagecoach, 1992
93ABY	Leyland Tiger TRCTL11/3R	Berkhof Everest 370	C53F	1986	Ex Abbey, Sheffield, 1993
D124TFT	Freight Rover Sherpa 365	Carlyle	B18F	1986	Ex Collingwood, Wheatley Hill, 1992
D833KWT	Freight Rover Sherpa 365	Dormobile	DP16F	1987	Ex West Riding, 1990
D838KWT	Freight Rover Sherpa 365	Dormobile	DP16F	1987	Ex West Riding, 1990
G754JET	Mercedes-Benz L408D	Whittaker	M15	1989	
K757PUT	Toyota Coaster HDB30R	Caetano Optimo II	C21F	1992	

Livery: White and red

Previous Registrations:

93ABY	C151SPB	XGB63W	HSP593W, 4585SC

The newest full-size coach in the Hennings fleet is a Leyland Tiger with Berkhof Everest bodywork. The Everest, at 3.7 metres, was probably the tallest single-deck coach of its time. The name, therefore, was aptly choosen. 93ABY was new to the Green Line operation and was originally registered C151SPB. It is seen at William Street Coach Park in Scarborough. *David Little*

HENRY COOPER

L & G Greaves, Lane End Garage, Annitsford, Tyne & Wear

JCN581N	Bedford YRQ	Duple Dominant	C45F	1975	
TBR527V	Leyland Leopard PSU3E/4R	Duple Dominant	B55F	1979	Ex United, 1993
JFT412X	Bedford YMQ	Duple Dominant III	C45F	1981	
WCN112Y	Bedford YNT	Duple Laser	C53F	1983	
ESU110	Volvo B10M-61	Plaxton Paramount 3500 II	C49FT	1986	
671MBB	Volvo B10M-61	Plaxton Paramount 3500 III	C49FT	1988	
OBR297	Volvo B10M-61	Plaxton Paramount 3500 III	C51FT	1989	

Livery: Brown and cream

Previous Registrations:

671MBB	E967ECN	OBR297	From new
ESU110	C417OTN	WCN112Y	VVK608Y, 671MBB

Henry Cooper, also known as Cooper's of Annitsford, operates a small fleet of coaches in a livery of two-tone brown and cream. JFT412X is a Bedford YMQ with Duple Dominant III bodywork, an unusual combination, and is seen in the lane adjacent to the operator's garage. *David Little*

HUNTERS (Seaton Delaval)

H W Hunter & Sons (Seaton Delaval) Ltd, Westbourne Garage, Seaton Delaval,
Whitley Bay, Tyne & Wear, NE25 0BE

78	C432SJU	Ford Transit 150	Robin Hood	B16F	1985	Ex Midland Red North, 1991
79	C453BHY	Ford Transit 150	Dormobile	B16F	1986	Ex City Line, 1989
80	D552MOK	Ford Transit 150	Carlyle	B16F	1986	Ex Stamford Vale, 1989
81	UNA859S	Leyland Atlantean AN68A/1R	Park Royal	H43/32F	1977	Ex GM Buses, 1990
82	ANC917T	Leyland Atlantean AN68A/1R	Park Royal	H43/32F	1978	Ex GM Buses, 1990
86	YNL218V	Leyland Atlantean AN68A/2R	MCW	H49/37F	1979	Ex Go-Ahead Northern, 1991
89	KUB542V	Leyland Leopard PSU3E/4R	Plaxton Supreme IV Express	C49F	1979	Ex Bedminster Coaches, 1991
91	VFT184T	Leyland Atlantean AN68/2R	MCW	H49/37F	1979	Ex Go-Ahead Northern, 1991
92	EDZ215	Leyland Tiger TRCTL11/2R	Plaxton Paramount 3200 E	C53F	1983	Ex NDY, Quarrington Hill, 1992
93	UUM77R	Leyland Leopard PSU3C/4R	Plaxton Supreme III Express	C53F	1977	Ex South Yorkshire, Pontefract, 1992
94	OWJ165X	Leyland Leopard PSU3G/4R	Eastern Coach Works B51	C49F	1981	Ex Busways, 1992
95	OWJ166X	Leyland Leopard PSU3G/4R	Eastern Coach Works B51	C49F	1981	Ex Busways, 1992
96	THH615S	Leyland Leopard PSU3E/4R	Duple Dominant I	DP53F	1977	Ex Escort, Middlesborough, 1993
97	BKR835Y	Leyland Leopard PSU3G/4R	Eastern Coach Works B51	C49F	1982	Ex East Kent, 1993
98	UKE828X	Leyland Leopard PSU3G/4R	Eastern Coach Works B51	DP49F	1982	Ex East Kent, 1993

Livery: Cream and maroon

Previous Registrations:
EDZ215   RMO203Y

In recent months Hunters of Seaton Delaval has reduced double deck numbers to just four examples. Their replacements are Leyland Leopards, the latest arrivals having Eastern Coach Works bodies. The PSU3G chassis variant was the final one in an illustrious line. New to East Kent, 97 (BKR835Y) is seen operating service 811 to Cramlington. *Bill Potter*

HUNTER'S (Tantobie)

Hunter Bros (Tantobie) Ltd, The Garage, 19 Johnson Terrace, Tantobie, Co Durham.

VWY845L	Bedford YRQ	Plaxton Elite III	C45F	1973	Ex Baddeley, Holmfirth, 1976
RUP906M	Bedford YRT	Duple Dominant	C53F	1974	
JUP189T	Bedford YMT	Duple Dominant	B55F	1978	
WPT445V	Bedford YMT	Duple Dominant II	C53F	1980	
GVK820W	Bedford YMQ	Duple Dominant	B47F	1980	
PNM695W	Bedford YMQ-S	Duple Dominant II	C35F	1981	Ex Tourmaster, Loughborough, 1984
NDW137X	Leyland Tiger TRCTL11/2R	Plaxton Supreme V Express	C53F	1982	Ex Hill's, Tredegar, 1986
D341APG	Mercedes-Benz 609D	Reeve Burgess	B20F	1987	Ex Taylor, West End, 1990

Livery: White and black

The only midibus in the fleet of Hunter of Tantobie is D341APG which has a Reeve Burgess coachbuilt body fitted on a Mercedes-Benz 609D chassis-cowl. This was probably one of the last bodies built at Chesterfield before the standard midibus product was christened the Beaver. It is seen at the former terminus of Hunter's 713 route. *David Little*

JOLLY

W H Jolly, Field Cottage, South Hylton, Sunderland, Tyne & Wear.

Depot: Union Street Garage, South Hylton

BBR736S	Bedford YMT	Duple Dominant	B53F	1977
LGR45T	Bedford YLQ	Duple Dominant II	C45F	1978
LGR46T	Bedford YLQ	Duple Dominant II	C45F	1978
LGR47T	Bedford YLQ	Duple Dominant II	C45F	1978
BGR683W	Bedford YMT	Duple Dominant	B53F	1980
BGR684W	Bedford YMT	Duple Dominant	B53F	1980
KTY23X	Bedford YMT	Duple Dominant	B53F	1981
KTY24X	Bedford YMT	Duple Dominant	B53F	1981

Livery: Fawn and brown

Jolly's fleet has remained unchanged for ten years and is based entirely on the Bedford/Duple combination which was the backbone of the fleet for many established independents. Dominant bus bodywork is carried by KTY24X here departing Sunderland city centre for home. *Phillip Stephenson*

KINGSLEY COACHES

D Kingsley, Unit G, Pensway Way, Portobello Industrial Estate, Birtley,
Tyne & Wear, DH3 2SA

JJG1P	Leyland Atlantean AN68/1R	Eastern Coach Works	H43/30F	1976	Ex East Kent, 1992
JJG9P	Leyland Atlantean AN68/1R	Eastern Coach Works	H43/30F	1976	Ex East Kent, 1992
KJD19P	Leyland Fleetline FE30ALR(6LXB) MCW		H44/32F	1976	Ex Trent, 1992
KUC991P	Leyland Fleetline FE30ALR(6LXB) MCW		H44/32F	1976	Ex Trent, 1992
SHJ886R	Bedford VAS5	Plaxton Supreme III	C29F	1976	Ex Martindale, Shildon, 1992
RJU405R	Bedford YRT	Plaxton Supreme III	C53F	1977	Ex Shaw, Craghead, 1988
YTU320S	Leyland Leopard PSU3E/4R	Duple Dominant I	C49F	1977	Ex C-Line, 1991
UVK868T	Bedford YLQ	Duple Dominant	C45F	1978	Ex Wear Valley Training, Crook, 1991
CBB467V	Bedford YMT	Duple Dominant II Express	C53F	1980	Ex Busways, 1990
CBB469V	Bedford YMT	Duple Dominant II Express	C53F	1980	Ex Busways, 1990
TOI1603	MAN SR280	MAN	C46FT	1980	Ex Elliott, Ware, 1992
C132CFB	MCW Metroliner HR131/7	MCW	C48FT	1986	Ex Wessex, 1993

Livery: Red and white

Previous Registrations:

TOI1603	WCO740V

Kingsley Coaches operates a variety of coaches and double deckers on school contracts and Tyne and Wear PTE tendered workings. JJG1P is seen at Kingsley's Birtley depot early in 1993. The 'TW PTE bus' board at the bottom right hand corner of the windscreen is to show that the bus operates on a contract service for the executive.
David Little

LEVEN VALLEY

P W Thompson, 55 Marwood Drive, Great Ayton, North Yorkshire, TS9 6PD

NWL653M	Ford R1014	Willowbrook 001	B45F	1973	Ex Balfour Beatty, 1987
H675ATN	Toyota Coaster HB31	Caetano Optimo	C21F	1990	
H312BGD	Mercedes-Benz 709D	Dormobile Routemaker	B29F	1991	
J916HGD	Peugeot-Talbot Pullman	Talbot	B22F	1991	Ex Argyll, Greenock, 1992
J219HDS	Ford Transit VE6	Ford	M16	1992	
K396NGG	Mercedes-Benz 709D	Dormobile Routemaker	B29F	1992	
L923VGA	Mercedes-Benz 709D	Dormobile Routemaker	B29F	1993	

Livery: White or yellow

Named vehicles: NWL653M *Sir Rocky Roland;* H675ATN *Avalon;* H312BGD *St Michael;* J916HGD *Merlin;* J219HDS *Astraea;* K396NGG *St Patrick;* L923VGA *Chiron.*

Leven Valley operates a mixture of commercial and tendered services in the Cleveland area. Dormobile-bodied Mercedes-Benz 609D, H312BGD, is in Stockton High Street about to operate Cleveland County Council tendered service 572 from Stockton to Middlesbrough. The vehicle was registered by the dealer, Blythswood, in Glasgow . They are currently a significant supplier of product frm the revitalised coach builder now known as Dormobile. *David Little*

MARTINDALES

Martindale Coaches Ltd, 2 North Street, Ferryhill, Co Durham, DL17 8HX

GAN743J	Leyland Leopard PSU3B/4RT	Plaxton Elite II	C53F	1971	Ex Wood, Blackpool, 1987
TUP77K	Leyland Leopard PSU5/4RT	Plaxton Elite II	C57F	1972	Ex Derwent, Swalwell, 1979
NWW222K	Leyland Leopard PSU3B/4RT	Plaxton Elite II	C53F	1972	Ex Longster, Pateley Br, 1975
CUP235L	Leyland Leopard PSU3B/4R	Plaxton Elite III Express	C53F	1973	
MJH277L	Leyland Leopard PSU3B/4R	Plaxton Elite III	C53F	1973	Ex Florence, Morecambe, 1987
AGM671L	Leyland Leopard PSU3/3R	Alexander AYS	B53F	1973	Ex Tyne & Wear Omnibus, 1988
AGM687L	Leyland Leopard PSU3/3R	Alexander AYS	B53F	1973	Ex Trimdon MS, 1988
NPT82M	Leyland Leopard PSU3B/4R	Duple Dominant	DP51F	1973	Ex Fir Tree, Crook, 1980
RBU201M	Leyland Leopard PSU3B/4R	Plaxton Elite III	C51F	1974	Ex Florence, Morecambe, 1987
PPT400P	Leyland Leopard PSU5A/4R	Plaxton Supreme III	C57F	1976	
WPT393R	Leyland Leopard PSU3C/4R	Plaxton Supreme III	C53F	1977	
OPT654T	Leyland Leopard PSU5C/4R	Plaxton Supreme III	C57F	1979	
VPT101V	Leyland Leopard PSU3E/4R	Plaxton Supreme IV Express	C53F	1980	
VPT102V	Leyland Leopard PSU3E/4R	Plaxton Supreme IV Express	C53F	1980	
LEF459W	Leyland Leopard PSU5C/4R	Plaxton Supreme IV	C48F	1981	
LEF460W	Leyland Leopard PSU5C/4R	Plaxton Supreme IV Express	C51F	1981	
910UPG	Volvo B10M-61	Jonckheere Jubilee P90	CH51/9FT	1984	Ex SUT, 1987
ESU981	Volvo B10M-53	Jonckheere Jubilee P95	CH56/5FT	1986	
D841EVN	Scania K112TRB	Plaxton Paramount 4000 II	CH53/14CT	1987	
E927MAJ	Scania K112TRB	Plaxton Paramount 4000 II	CH51/16FT	1988	
F173DET	Scania K112CRB	Plaxton Paramount 3500 III	C51FT	1989	
F174DET	Scania K112CRB	Plaxton Paramount 3500 III	C51FT	1989	
F175DET	Scania K92CRB	Plaxton P'mount 3200 (1991)	C49FT	1989	
G28HKY	Scania K113TRB	Plaxton Paramount 4000 III	CH51/16CT	1990	
G29HKY	Scania K113TRB	Plaxton Paramount 4000 III	CH51/16CT	1990	
G30HKY	Scania K113TRB	Plaxton Paramount 4000 III	CH51/16CT	1990	

Liveries: Maroon, red and cream; Sun Travel - G28HKY.

Previous Registrations:

ESU981	C731YEF	910UPG	A320XHE

Martindales continue to operate a large number of Leyland Leopards with many body types respresented in the fleet. NWW222K has a Plaxton Elite II body and is seen at Martindales' Ferryhill depot. Remarkably, for a vehicle of this age, it is with only its second owner.
David Little

MICHAEL FRANKS

C Franks, 7 Attlee Crescent, Haswell Plough, County Durham, DH6 2GN

Depot: Don Smith coach depot, Murton

JOX469P	Leyland Leopard PSU3C/4R	Plaxton Supreme III Express	C49F	1976	Ex Holdcore, Peterlee, 1992
SUR279R	Leyland Leopard PSU3C/4R	Plaxton Supreme III	C53F	1977	Ex Redline, Wheatley Hill, 1990
ROU349S	Leyland Leopard PSU3E/4R	Plaxton Supreme III Express	C49F	1977	Ex Badgerline, 1992
DGR15S	Leyland Leopard PSU3E/4R	Plaxton Supreme III	C53F	1978	Ex Watson's, Annfield Plain, 1987
JMB333T	Leyland Leopard PSU3E/4R	Duple Dominant II	C49F	1979	Ex McConnachie, Pt.Glasgow'89
AGR229W	Leyland Leopard PSU3F/4R	Willowbrook 003	C49F	1980	Ex Northumbria, 1992

Livery: Red and white

A vehicle with a varied past, Leyland Leopard JOX469P was new to Midland Red in 1976. It passed to Midland Red North on the break-up of the company in 1981 and operated for varying periods as a coach and a bus. The door arrangement of the Plaxton Supreme III Express can be seen in this view, taken during the 1993 summer in Sunderland. Michael Franks now operates a fleet consisting entirely of Leyland Leopards, having replaced the Leyland Nationals used previously. *Bill Potter*

MILL COACHES

L E Curnow, Hobson Service Station, Burnopfield, County Durham

NWL651M	Ford R1014	Willowbrook 001	B45F	1973	Ex Alderson, Bowes, 1992
IIL4295	Leyland Leopard PSU3E/4R	Duple Dominant II	C53F	1977	Ex NDY, Quarrington Hill, 1993
YPL94T	AEC Reliance 6U2R	Duple Dominant II Express	C49F	1979	Ex Gilchrist, East Kilbride, 1990
VSH71V	Bedford YMT	Duple Dominant II Express	C53F	1979	Ex Dodds, Ashington, 1992
A528UTC	Bova EL26/581	Bova Europa	C49F	1983	Ex Majestic, Cheslyn Hay, 1988
HIL3086	Bova FHD12.280	Bova Futura	C49FT	1985	Ex Boyden, Castle Donington, 1991

Livery: Red and cream

Previous Registrations:

A528UTC	TJT906		HIL3086	B330ORY, TRB1	IIL4295	RYL715R

New to the Green Line operation, YPL94T is an AEC Reliance with Duple Dominant II Express bodywork. Now with Mill Coaches it works with similarly bodied vehicles based on Leyland and Bedford chassis. *David Little*

MOOR-DALE

Moor-Dale Coaches Ltd, 7 Old Eldon Square, Newcastle-upon-Tyne,
Tyne & Wear, NE1 7JG

Moor-Dale Coaches Ltd is an autonomous subsidiary of the Proudmutual Group.

10	GIL8489	Volvo B10M-61	Plaxton Paramount 3500	C53F	1984	Ex R & M, Hexham, 1993
11	UPP938	Volvo B10M-61	Plaxton Paramount 3500 II	C53FT	1985	
13	GIL7547	Volvo B10M-61	Plaxton Paramount 3500 III	C49FT	1987	Ex Excelsior, 1991
14	GIL6949	Volvo B10M-61	Plaxton Paramount 3500 III	C49F	1987	Ex Wallace Arnold, 1991
15	GIL6253	Volvo B10M-61	Plaxton Paramount 3500 III	C53F	1987	Ex Wallace Arnold, 1991
16	D271XRG	Volvo B10M-61	Plaxton Paramount 3500 III	C57F	1987	
17	JVJ529	Volvo B10M-61	Plaxton Paramount 3500 III	C49FT	1987	
18	E472BTN	Volvo B10M-61	Duple 320	C57F	1987	
19	HIL7591	Volvo B10M-61	Plaxton Paramount 3500 III	C49F	1987	
20	HIL7592	Volvo B10M-61	Duple 340	C51FT	1988	
21	HIL7593	Volvo B10M-61	Duple 340	C51FT	1988	
22	HIL7594	Volvo B10M-61	Plaxton Paramount 3500 III	C53FT	1987	Ex Shearings, 1992
23	HIL7595	Volvo B10M-61	Plaxton Paramount 3500 III	C53FT	1987	Ex Shearings, 1992
24	HIL7597	Volvo B10M-61	Plaxton Paramount 3500 III	C53FT	1987	Ex Shearings, 1992
31	F381NVK	Volvo B10M-60	Plaxton Paramount 3500 III	C49F	1989	
32	G382UNL	Volvo B10M-60	Berkhof Excellence 2000	C53FT	1990	
33	H383DBB	Volvo B10M-60	Berkhof Excellence 2000	C53FT	1991	
34	K384RJR	Volvo B10M-60	Berkhof Excellence 2000	C53FT	1993	
42	AGR233W	Leyland Leopard PSU3F/4R	Willowbrook 003	C49F	1980	Ex Northumbria, 1992
45	RVN249X	Leyland Leopard PSU3F/4R	Willowbrook 003	C49F	1982	Ex Northumbria, 1992
52	YUH116T	Bedford YMT	Plaxton Supreme IV	C53F	1979	Ex Northumbria, 1990
66	E677DCU	Leyland Lynx LX112L10ZR1R	Leyland	B51F	1987	
67	E678DCU	Leyland Lynx LX112L10ZR1R	Leyland	B51F	1987	
73	K73SRG	Dennis Dart 9.8SDL3017	Plaxton Pointer	B43F	1993	
74	K74SRG	Dennis Dart 9.8SDL3017	Plaxton Pointer	B43F	1993	
75	K75SRG	Dennis Dart 9.8SDL3017	Plaxton Pointer	B43F	1993	
80	JPL132K	Leyland Atlantean PDR1A/1Sp	Park Royal	H43/29D	1972	Ex Kentish Bus, 1991
81	JPL138K	Leyland Atlantean PDR1A/1Sp	Park Royal	H43/29D	1972	Ex Kentish Bus, 1991
83	SCD735N	Leyland Atlantean AN68/1R	Park Royal	H43/30F	1974	Ex Kentish Bus, 1992
84	SUF140N	Leyland Atlantean AN68/1R	Park Royal	H43/30F	1974	Ex Kentish Bus, 1992

Livery: Red, blue and white (buses); silver, grey and red (coaches).

Previous Registrations:

GIL6253	D209LWX	HIL7591	D270XRG	HIL7595	E663UNE		
GIL6949	D210LWX	HIL7592	E179FFT	HIL7597	E660UNE		
GIL7547	D481KJT	HIL7593	E180FFT	JVJ529	D269XRG		
GIL8489	A645GLD	HIL7594	E662UNE	UPP938	B368HNL		

The newest coaches in the Moor-Dale fleet are Berkhof-bodied Volvo B10Ms. The Excellence range of bodies from Berkhof were introduced into the UK after the Dutch coachbuilder had been absent from the market for a short period in the late 1980s. Showing off the 2000 design is 32 (G382UNL). *David Little*

Moor-Dale's Leyland Lynx are usually employed on the Dudley Circle services 350/351 and 67 (E678DCU) demonstrates this. It is one of a pair fitted with Cummins engines and represents the growing investment in stage carriage vehicles by this operator. *Bill Potter*

The latest deliveries to the Moor-Dale fleet are three Dennis Darts fitted with DiPTAC specification features. These Plaxton-bodied vehicles comply with tender requirements and can normally be found on services 365 and 366. No.74 (K74SRG) is seen on the latter to Cramlington. *Bill Potter*

Moor-Dale's double deckers are normally only used on school services plus the occasional private hire. Formerly with Kentish Bus, Park Royal-bodied Leyland Atlantean JPL138K was at Four Lane Ends Metro station when double deckers often worked service M63. *David Little*

NORTH RIDER

E C Ward and W Wooldridge, 10 Dearham Grove, Cramlington,
Northumberland, NE23 9FR

1	MIW1239	Leyland Leopard PSU3E/4R	Duple Dominant II Express	C53F	1980	Ex South Yorkshire's, Transport 1991
2	MIW1241	Mercedes-Benz L608D	Whittaker	C19F	1985	Ex Owen, Chapelhall, 1991
3	C240GTU	Iveco Daily 49.10	Robin Hood City Nippy	B21F	1986	Ex GM Buses, 1992
4	D507MJA	Iveco Daily 49.10	Robin Hood City Nippy	B19F	1987	Ex GM Buses, 1992
5	D525MJA	Iveco Daily 49.10	Robin Hood City Nippy	B19F	1987	Ex GM Buses, 1992
6	IIL4597	DAF MB200DKTL600	Van Hool Alizée	C50FT	1983	Ex Butler, Kirkby, 1993
7	F900XOE	Iveco Daily 49.10	Carlyle Dailybus 2	B25F	1989	Ex Trent, 1993

Previous Registrations:

IIL4597	68BUT		MIW1239	GTG633W		MIW1241	C407GET

Livery: Green and white

North Rider is a newcomer to bus operation in the Tyneside area, using a livery of white and bottle green. Routes operated include a tendered midibus service from Four Lane Ends Metro station and a rural service from Hexham to Consett. Photographed working the former is 4 (D507MJA), an Iveco Daily that originated with GM Buses where it was one of 229 similar vehicles put into service during 1986 and 1987. *Keith Grimes*

NORTHUMBRIA

Northumbria Motor Services Ltd, 6 Portland Terrace, Jesmond,
Newcastle upon Tyne, Tyne & Wear, NE2 1QQ

Northumbria is an autonomous subsidiary of the Proudmutual Group.
Depots: Lisburn Street, Alnwick; Lintonville Terrace, Ashington; Bridge Street, Blyth; Marygate, Berwick; Gallowgate, Newcastle; Burn Lane, Hexham; Jesmond Road, Newcastle; Dark Lane, Morpeth and Park Avenue, Whitley Bay.

101	HKR11	MCW MetroRider MF154/2	MCW	C28F	1988	Ex Boro'line, 1992
108	OSK775	Bova EL26/581	Bova Europa	C45FT	1984	Ex United, 1987
111	FSU346	Bova FHD12.280	Bova Futura	C49FT	1985	Ex Kentish Bus, 1985
112	NMS700	Bova FHD12.280	Bova Futura	C48FT	1990	Ex Boyden, Castle Donington, 1991
113	OSU894	Bova FHD12.290	Bova Futura	C49FT	1988	
114	OSU895	Bova FHD12.290	Bova Futura	C49FT	1988	
115	WSV570	Bova FHD12.290	Bova Futura	C49FT	1988	Ex Black Horse, London, 1990
116	GSU346	Bova FHD12.290	Bova Futura	C49FT	1988	Ex Black Horse, London, 1990
118	GSU348	Bova FHD12.290	Bova Futura	C49FT	1988	Ex Black Horse, London, 1990
119	NMS100	Bova FHD12.290	Bova Futura	C49FT	1990	
120	J20NMS	Bova FHD12.290	Bova Futura	C49FT	1992	
121	K121HWF	Bova FHD12.290	Bova Futura	C49FT	1993	
130	GSU347	Bova FHD12.290	Bova Futura	C47FT	1991	Ex Black Horse, London, 1990
131	K131FKW	Bova FHD12.290	Bova Futura	C46FT	1993	
132	K132FKW	Bova FHD12.290	Bova Futura	C46FT	1993	

Many of Northumbria's Bova Futura coaches are in a livery which can accomodate changes of name by the addition of vinyls. Seen working a contract for Blue Chip Travel, and carrying its scheme, is 114 (OSU895). Originally registered E114GBB, this distinctive vehicle is seen on Buckingham Palace Road at the end of January 1993. *Colin Lloyd*

158	NMS789	MCW Metroliner DR130/6	MCW	CH55/19DT	1985	Ex North Devon, 1987
159	WSV572	MCW Metroliner DR130/6	MCW	CH55/19DT	1985	Ex North Devon, 1987
160	WSV571	MCW Metroliner DR130/10	MCW	CH55/17DT	1985	Ex United, 1987
164	WSV573	MCW Metroliner DR130/19	MCW	CH55/16DT	1986	Ex London & Country, 1991
193	WLT859	MCW Metroliner DR130/33	MCW	CH53/14DT	1987	Ex Eastern Scottish, 1990
201	BBR996S	Leyland Leopard PSU5C/4R	Plaxton Supreme III	C50F	1978	Ex United, 1986
202	BBR997S	Leyland Leopard PSU5C/4R	Plaxton Supreme III	C50F	1978	Ex United, 1986

203-207

		Leyland Leopard PSU3E/4RT	Duple 320(1987)	C55F	1977-78	Ex United, 1986

203	WSV565	204	WSV566	205	WSV567	206	WSV568	207	WSV569

208	LGR411T	Leyland Leopard PSU3E/4R	Plaxton Supreme III Express	C49F	1978	Ex United, 1986
209	LGR413T	Leyland Leopard PSU3E/4R	Plaxton Supreme III Express	C49F	1979	Ex United, 1986
210	JUP114T	Leyland Leopard PSU5C/4R	Plaxton Supreme III	C51F	1979	Ex United, 1986
211	JUP115T	Leyland Leopard PSU5C/4R	Plaxton Supreme III	C51F	1979	Ex United, 1986
212	SPT216V	Leyland Leopard PSU3E/4R	Plaxton Supreme IV Express	C49F	1979	Ex United, 1986
213	SPT217V	Leyland Leopard PSU3E/4R	Plaxton Supreme IV Express	C49F	1979	Ex United, 1986
214	SPT218V	Leyland Leopard PSU3E/4R	Plaxton Supreme IV Express	C49F	1979	Ex United, 1986
223	NDC238W	Leyland Leopard PSU3F/4R	Plaxton Supreme IV Express	C49F	1981	Ex United, 1986
224	RVN245X	Leyland Leopard PSU3F/4R	Willowbrook 003	C47F	1982	Ex United, 1986
225	RVN246X	Leyland Leopard PSU3F/4R	Willowbrook 003	C47F	1982	Ex United, 1986
226	RVN248X	Leyland Leopard PSU3F/4R	Willowbrook 003	C47F	1982	Ex United, 1986
228	RVN250X	Leyland Leopard PSU3F/4R	Willowbrook 003	C47F	1982	Ex United, 1986

229-233

		Leyland Leopard PSU3F/4R	Plaxton Supreme IV Express	C49F	1981	Ex United, 1986

229	NDC501W	230	NDC502W	231	NDC503W	232	NDC504W	233	NDC505W

The number of MCW Metroliners used by Northumbria on National Express Rapide contracts is reducing. This is in common with most other operators of the type, as more emphasis is placed on 46-seaters for the National Express network. No.164 (WSV573) was originally C139ALJ when new to Shamrock & Rambler and is seen at Gallowgate Coach Station, Newcastle. *Steve Warburton*

234	PUP624T	Leyland Leopard PSU5C/4R	Plaxton Supreme IV	C51F	1979	Ex United, 1986
235	PPT823T	Leyland Leopard PSU5C/4R	Plaxton Supreme IV	C51F	1979	Ex United, 1986
236	SUP326V	Leyland Leopard PSU5C/4R	Plaxton Supreme IV	C51F	1979	Ex United, 1986
237	SUP727V	Leyland Leopard PSU5C/4R	Plaxton Supreme IV	C51F	1979	Ex United, 1986
238	GDF277V	Leyland Leopard PSU5C/4R	Duple Dominant II	C53F	1979	Ex Kentish Bus, 1991
239	SND296X	Leyland Leopard PSU5D/4R	Plaxton Supreme V	C53F	1981	Ex Kentish Bus, 1991
240	YEL97Y	Leyland Leopard PSU5E/4R	Eastern Coach Works B51	C50F	1983	Ex Kentish Bus, 1991
241	YEL98Y	Leyland Leopard PSU5E/4R	Eastern Coach Works B51	C50F	1983	Ex Kentish Bus, 1991
242	B262KPF	Leyland Tiger TRCTL11/2RH	Plaxton Paramount 3200	C51F	1985	Ex Kentish Bus, 1992
243	B265KPF	Leyland Tiger TRCTL11/2RH	Plaxton Paramount 3200	C51F	1985	Ex Kentish Bus, 1992
244	B273KPF	Leyland Tiger TRCTL11/2RH	Plaxton Paramount 3200	C51F	1985	Ex Kentish Bus, 1992
245	B279KPF	Leyland Tiger TRCTL11/3RH	Plaxton Paramount 3200	C51F	1985	Ex Kentish Bus, 1992
246	B276KPF	Leyland Tiger TRCTL11/3RH	Plaxton Paramount 3200	C51F	1985	Ex Kentish Bus, 1992
247	B277KPF	Leyland Tiger TRCTL11/3RH	Plaxton Paramount 3200	C51F	1985	Ex Kentish Bus, 1992

Thirsk was one of the stopping points for a Northumbria excursion worked by 207 (WSV569). This Leyland Leopard was re-bodied in 1987 with a Duple 320 body intended to extend the working-life of the chassis. Operators are examining again the concept of re-bodying quality chassis for further use especially since the removal of bus grants, and the steady rise in vehicle prices has accelerated this practice where opportunity permits. *David Donati*

Many local or short-distance express services in Northumberland are operated by Northumbria's fleet of Leyland Leopard and Tiger coaches. Eastern Coach Works-bodied 240 (YEL97Y), in Blyth, operating service 447 to Morpeth is one of the last of the long line of Leopard chassis variants which commenced with the L1 type at the end of the 1950s. *G R Mills*

251-267

DAF SB220LC550 · Optare Delta · DP48F · 1989-90

251	G251SRG	255	G255UVK	259	H259CFT	262	H262CFT	265	H265CFT
252	G252SRG	256	G256UVK	260	H598CNL	263	H263CFT	266	H266CFT
253	G253SRG	257	G257UVK	261	H261CFT	264	H264CFT	267	H267CFT
254	G254SRG	258	G258UVK						

301	C263XEF	Leyland Olympian ONLXB/1R	Eastern Coach Works	DPH43/29F	1986	Ex United, 1986
302	C264XEF	Leyland Olympian ONLXB/1R	Eastern Coach Works	DPH43/29F	1986	Ex United, 1986

303-312

Leyland Olympian ONCL10/2RZ Alexander RH · DPH43/33F · 1988

303	F303JTY	305	F305JTY	307	F307JTY	309	F309JTY	311	F311JTY
304	F304JTY	306	F306JTY	308	F308JTY	310	F310JTY	312	F312JTY

313	C616ANW	Leyland Olympian ONTL11/1R	Eastern Coach Works	DPH41/32F	1986	Ex West Riding, 1993
314	C617ANW	Leyland Olympian ONTL11/1R	Eastern Coach Works	DPH41/32F	1986	Ex West Riding, 1993
341	EEH901Y	Leyland Olympian ONLXB/1R	Eastern Coach Works	DPH41/32F	1983	Ex Kentish Bus, 1990
342	EEH908Y	Leyland Olympian ONLXB/1R	Eastern Coach Works	DPH41/32F	1983	Ex Kentish Bus, 1990
343	SPY205X	Leyland Olympian ONLXB/1R	Eastern Coach Works	DPH41/32F	1982	Ex United, 1986
344	SPY210X	Leyland Olympian ONLXB/1R	Eastern Coach Works	DPH41/32F	1982	Ex United, 1986
345	WDC212Y	Leyland Olympian ONLXB/1R	Eastern Coach Works	DPH41/32F	1982	Ex United, 1986
346	SPY204X	Leyland Olympian ONLXB/1R	Eastern Coach Works	DPH41/32F	1982	Ex United, 1986
352	A102FPL	Leyland Olympian ONTL11/2R	Eastern Coach Works	CH45/27F	1984	Ex Kentish Bus, 1988
353	OSK774	Leyland Olympian ONTL11/2R	Northern Counties(1992)	DPH47/30F	1984	Ex Kentish Bus, 1988
356	C211UPD	Leyland Olympian ONTL11/2RSp	Eastern Coach Works	CH45/28F	1986	Ex County, 1990
357	C212UPD	Leyland Olympian ONTL11/2RSp	Eastern Coach Works	CH45/28F	1986	Ex County, 1990
358	C213UPD	Leyland Olympian ONTL11/2RSp	Eastern Coach Works	CH45/28F	1986	Ex County, 1990
359	C448BKM	Leyland Olympian ONTL11/2R	Eastern Coach Works	CH45/28F	1985	Ex Maidstone & District, 1990
360	C449BKM	Leyland Olympian ONTL11/2R	Eastern Coach Works	CH45/28F	1985	Ex Maidstone & District, 1990
361	C450BKM	Leyland Olympian ONTL11/2R	Eastern Coach Works	CH45/28F	1985	Ex Maidstone & District, 1990
362	C451BKM	Leyland Olympian ONTL11/2R	Eastern Coach Works	CH45/28F	1985	Ex Maidstone & District, 1990
363	C452GKE	Leyland Olympian ONTL11/2R	Eastern Coach Works	CH45/28F	1986	Ex Maidstone & District, 1990
364	C453GKE	Leyland Olympian ONTL11/2R	Eastern Coach Works	CH45/28F	1986	Ex Maidstone & District, 1990
365	C454GKE	Leyland Olympian ONTL11/2R	Eastern Coach Works	CH45/28F	1986	Ex Maidstone & District, 1990
366	C214UPD	Leyland Olympian ONTL11/2RSp	Eastern Coach Works	CH45/26F	1986	Ex County, 1991
367	C215UPD	Leyland Olympian ONTL11/2RSp	Eastern Coach Works	CH45/26F	1986	Ex County, 1991
368	B697BPU	Leyland Olympian ONTL11/2RSp	Eastern Coach Works	CH45/28F	1985	Ex Eastern National, 1992

401-409

Leyland Olympian ONLXB/1R · Eastern Coach Works · H44/32F · 1982 · Ex United, 1986

401	SPY201X	402	SPY202X	403	SPY203X	407	WDC211Y	409	WDC213Y

431	C259UAJ	Leyland Olympian ONLXB/1R	Eastern Coach Works	H45/32F	1985	Ex United, 1986
432	C260UAJ	Leyland Olympian ONLXB/1R	Eastern Coach Works	H45/32F	1985	Ex United, 1986
433	C261UAJ	Leyland Olympian ONLXB/1R	Eastern Coach Works	H45/32F	1985	Ex United, 1986
434	C262UAJ	Leyland Olympian ONLXB/1R	Eastern Coach Works	H45/32F	1985	Ex United, 1986
500	MCU98K	Leyland Atlantean PDR1A/1RSp	Park Royal	O43/24D	1972	Ex Kentish Bus, 1989
501	MVK515R	Leyland Atlantean AN68A/2R	Alexander AL	H48/33F	1977	Ex Busways, 1992
502	MVK517R	Leyland Atlantean AN68A/2R	Alexander AL	H48/33F	1977	Ex Busways, 1992
503	MVK522R	Leyland Atlantean AN68A/2R	Alexander AL	H48/33F	1977	Ex Busways, 1992
526	BPT917S	Bristol VRT/SL3/6LXB	Eastern Coach Works	H43/31F	1977	Ex United, 1986
527	BPT918S	Bristol VRT/SL3/6LXB	Eastern Coach Works	H43/31F	1977	Ex United, 1986
530	BPT923S	Bristol VRT/SL3/6LXB	Eastern Coach Works	H42/31F	1977	Ex United, 1986
531	BPT924S	Bristol VRT/SL3/6LXB	Eastern Coach Works	H42/31F	1977	Ex Moor-Dale, 1991
533	BPT927S	Bristol VRT/SL3/6LXB	Eastern Coach Works	H43/31F	1977	Ex United, 1986
534	BPT928S	Bristol VRT/SL3/6LXB	Eastern Coach Works	H42/31F	1977	Ex United, 1986

536-554

Bristol VRT/SL3/6LXB · Eastern Coach Works · H43/31F* · 1978-79 · Ex United, 1986
*539/42/9/52 are H42/31F

536	CPT734S	541	CPT739S	544	DUP747S	548	HUP758T	552	HUP768T
538	CPT736S	542	CPT740S	546	DUP753S	549	HUP759T	553	OBR769T
539	CPT737S	543	DUP745S	547	HUP757T	551	HUP767T	554	OBR772T
540	CPT738S								

555	YCU961T	Bristol VRT/SL3/6LXB	Eastern Coach Works	O43/31F	1979	Ex United, 1986

Northumbria operate 17 Optare Deltas and all of these have high-back seating. No.255 (G255UVK) is seen in Newgate Street, Newcastle heading for its terminus at the Eldon Square bus concourse, built under the shopping centre.
G R Mills

The only double deckers delivered new to Northumbria are ten Leyland Olympians with Alexander bodies dating from 1988. Their sphere of operation often includes the express services between Newcastle and the Northumberland towns of Alnwick, Ashington and Blyth. Showing an electronic destination display, 307 (F307JTY) was leaving Haymarket bus station, Newcastle during May 1993. *Keith Grimes*

From the five Leyland Olympians with Eastern Coach Works coach bodies transferred to Northumbria by Kentish Bus in 1988 only two now remain. Of these, 353 (A103FPL) suffered a fire in which the body was destroyed and, during 1992, received a new body from Northern Counties. Subsequently registered OSK774 this vehicle was seen passing the Haymarket bus station in Newcastle on its regular route to Tynemouth. *Keith Grimes*

Midland Red North took delivery of ten Leyland Olympians with high-back seating in 1983, though two were sold to Kentish Bus in 1987. This pair have now moved to Northumbria where 341 (EEH901Y), first to arrive, is seen working service X18 to Alnwick. *G R Mills*

There are two open top buses in the Northumbria fleet, a standard Bristol VRT with Eastern Coach Works body and a Park Royal-bodied Leyland Atlantean. The appearance of the Atlantean on the open-top service from Whitley Bay to North Shields was uncommon, its normal work includes appearances at carnivals etc. Originally registered JPL110K, 500 (MCU98K) is seen in Newcastle performing promotional work for the Red Cross. *Steve Warburton*

The number of Eastern Coach Works-bodied Leyland Olympians in the Northumbria fleet was considerably reduced when 19 examples were transferred to Kentish Bus for use on London Regional Transport-tendered services. One of the remaining examples, 434 (C262UAJ), is seen in Newcastle. *Keith Grimes*

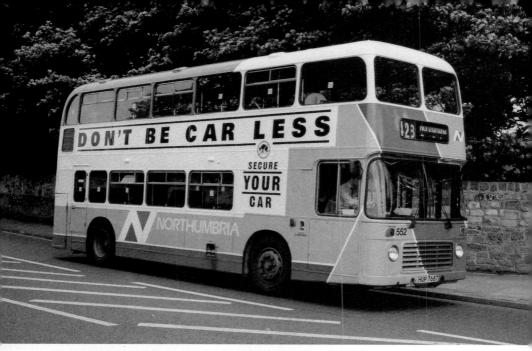

Above: **The mainstay of the double deck fleet was the Bristol VRT. The appearance of 552 (HUP768T) is altered by the use of plain glass instead of opening windows at the front of the upper deck. The vehicle pauses in Cramlington while heading for Newcastle, though Northumbria is displayed on the blind.** *Bill Potter*

Opposite, Top: **Northumbria have developed a coach fleet where the Bova Futura plays a dominant role. Identified by the bulbous frontal appearance, the Futura is used on tours and express work. Seen arriving at Victoria, London, is 113 (OSU894), one of many Northumbria vehicles that now carry cherished registration marks.** *Colin Lloyd.*

Opposite, Bottom: **Northumbria operate the Care Bus service for the Tyne & Wear PTE and have a Leyland National Greenway painted in the PTEs livery for this purpose. Originally a Gardner HLXC-engined Leyland National 2, 702 (XSV238) carried A141FDC when new to the United fleet, being transferred to Northumbria when that company was established in 1986.** *Keith Grimes*

The Daimler Fleetlines purchased from GM Buses are mostly confined to school contracts and miscellaneous workings. However, 598 (OBN505R) was photographed while on normal service at Blyth bus station.
G R Mills

556-572

	Bristol VRT/SL3/6LXB			Eastern Coach Works		H43/31F*	1979-80 Ex United, 1986	
							*557/61/2/4/6/7/72 are H42/31F	

556	OBR775T	559	SGR778V	562	SGR783V	565	SGR788V	569	SGR792V
557	OBR776T	560	SGR779V	563	SGR784V	566	SGR789V	570	SGR795V
558	SGR777V	561	SGR782V	564	SGR785V	567	SGR790V	572	SGR797V

573-591

	Bristol VRT/SL3/6LXB			Eastern Coach Works		H43/31F*	1980-81 Ex United, 1986	
							*576/88 are H42/31F; 577 rebodied 1980	

573	XPT798V	577	XPT803V	581	APT811W	586	APT819W	589	MEF826W
574	XPT799V	578	APT806W	583	APT816W	587	APT820W	590	PAJ827X
575	XPT800V	579	APT807W	584	APT817W	588	MEF825W	591	PAJ829X
576	XPT802V	580	APT810W	585	APT818W				

592-597

	Daimler Fleetline CRG6LXB			Northern Counties		H43/32F	1976 Ex GM Buses, 1987	

592	PRJ486R	594	PRJ489R	595	PRJ490R	596	PRJ492R	597	PRJ494R
593	PRJ488R							

598	OBN505R	Leyland Fleetline FE30AGR	Northern Counties	H45/32F	1977 Ex GM Buses, 1987
599	PTD639S	Leyland Fleetline FE30AGR	Northern Counties	H43/32F	1977 Ex GM Buses, 1987

615-630

	Bristol LH6L			Eastern Coach Works		B43F	1976-77 Ex United, 1986	

615	LGR655P	623	NGR683P	625	XPT686R	626	XUP693R	630	STO391R
622	NGR681P	624	NGR685P	627	SNU384R	629	SNU386R		

633-638

	Bristol LH6L			Eastern Coach Works		B43F	1979-80 Ex United, 1986	

633	LPT701T	635	LPT708T	636	MUP712T	637	MUP714T	638	AFB593V
634	LPT707T							

701	THX192S	Leyland National 10351A/2R		B25DL	1977 Ex London Buses, 1992
702	XSV238	Leyland National 2 NL116AHLXCT/1R E L Greenway (1992)		B23DL	1984 Ex United, 1986
710	NPK250R	Leyland National 10351A/1R		B41F	1977 Ex Kentish Bus, 1990
712	GOL399N	Leyland National 11351/1R		B49F	1975 Ex Midland Red North, 1987
714	GOL403N	Leyland National 11351/1R		B49F	1975 Ex Midland Red North, 1987
715	GOL404N	Leyland National 11351/1R		B49F	1975 Ex Midland Red North, 1987

Opposite, Top: In the mid 1980s the National Bus Company supplied several of its subsidiaries with the longer Leyland Olympian chassis fitted with an express version of the Eastern Coach Works body. At the time most were used on commuter services into London, with many now taking on other duties. Northumbrian's 367 (C215UPD), purchased for the Green Line operation, is typical and was photographed passing the Haymarket bus station in Newcastle. *Keith Grimes*

Opposite, Bottom: More than seven and a half thousand Leyland Nationals were built at Lillyhall in Cumbria, and the type is still the most common bus in service, though many are now with different operators. Northumbrian's 743 (NPK259R) was new to London Country before passing to the Northumbria sister company, Kentish Bus. It is of the shorter type, 10351A/1R, and is seen leaving Newcastle on a limited stop service to Blyth. *Keith Grimes*

Northumbria has purchased Leyland Nationals from a number of sources including Kentish Bus, Ribble, South Wales and, in the case of 714 (GOL403N), Midland Red North. The vehicle was photographed while heading out of Newcastle along Percy Street.
Steve Warburton

721	WPG217M	Leyland National 10351/1R/SC				DP39F	1974	Ex Kentish Bus, 1989	
722	XPD233N	Leyland National 10351/1R/SC				DP39F	1975	Ex Kentish Bus, 1989	
724	GPD296N	Leyland National 10351/1R/SC				DP39F	1975	Ex Kentish Bus, 1989	
726	LPB196P	Leyland National 10351/1R/SC				DP39F	1975	Ex Kentish Bus, 1989	
730	VPT944R	Leyland National 11351A/1R				B49F	1977	Ex United, 1986	
733	MHN131W	Leyland National 2 NL116L11/1R				B49F	1981	Ex United, 1986	
734	RDC735X	Leyland National 2 NL116L11/1R				B49F	1982	Ex United, 1986	
735	RDC736X	Leyland National 2 NL116L11/1R				B49F	1982	Ex United, 1986	

736-740
Leyland National 11351A/1R — B49F — 1976 — Ex South Wales, 1989

736	JTH763P	737	JTH765P	738	JTH777P	739	JTH778P	740	JTH781P

742	UPE208M	Leyland National 1051/1R				B41F	1974	Ex Kentish Bus, 1989	

743-750
Leyland National 10351A/1R — B41F — 1976-77 Ex Kentish Bus, 1989-90

743	NPK259R	744	NPK263R	747	NPK258R	749	SPC289R	750	UPB315S

756-774
Leyland National 11351A/1R — B49F — 1976-79 Ex United, 1986

756	SGR129R	763	CUP662S	766	JBR687T	772	LUP903T	774	RUP308V
758	ABR861S	764	CUP666S	769	JBR691T	773	PUP505T		

775-780
Leyland National 2 NL116AL11/1R — B49F — 1980 — Ex United 1986

775	UBR110V	777	APT120W	778	APT124W	779	APT125W	780	APT127W
776	UBR113V								

781-785
Leyland National 2 NL116AHLXCT/1R — B49F — 1983-84 Ex United 1986

781	A128FDC	782	A129FDC	783	A132FDC	784	A133FDC	785	A139FDC

787	NPK253R	Leyland National 10351A/1R	B41F	1976	Ex Kentish Bus, 1991
788	NPK257R	Leyland National 10351A/1R	B41F	1976	Ex Kentish Bus, 1991
789	SPC273R	Leyland National 10351A/1R	B41F	1977	Ex Kentish Bus, 1991
791	UPB333S	Leyland National 10351A/1R	B41F	1977	Ex Kentish Bus, 1991
792	YPF759T	Leyland National 10351A/1R	B41F	1978	Ex Kentish Bus, 1991
793	YPL399T	Leyland National 10351B/1R	B41F	1978	Ex Kentish Bus, 1991
794	YPL394T	Leyland National 10351B/1R	B41F	1978	Ex Kentish Bus, 1991
795	YPL412T	Leyland National 10351B/1R	B41F	1978	Ex Kentish Bus, 1991
796	BPL486T	Leyland National 10351B/1R	B41F	1979	Ex Kentish Bus, 1991
797	BPL476T	Leyland National 10351B/1R	B41F	1979	Ex Kentish Bus, 1991

801-845
MCW Metrorider MF150/27* — MCW — DP25F* — 1987 — *801-7/9 are MF150/21
*804/35/8/9/45 are B23F

801	E801BTN	811	E811BTN	820	E820BTN	829	E829BTN	838	E838BTN
802	E802BTN	812	E812BTN	821	E821BTN	830	E830BTN	839	E839BTN
803	E803BTN	813	E813BTN	822	E822BTN	831	E831BTN	840	E840BTN
804	E804BTN	814	E814BTN	823	E823BTN	832	E832BTN	841	E841BTN
805	E805BTN	815	E815BTN	824	E824BTN	833	E833BTN	842	E842BTN
806	E806BTN	816	E816BTN	825	E825BTN	834	E834BTN	843	E843BTN
807	E807BTN	817	E817BTN	826	E826BTN	835	E835BTN	844	E844BTN
809	E809BTN	818	E818BTN	827	E827BTN	836	E836BTN	845	E845BTN
810	E810BTN	819	E819BTN						

846	H840UUA	Optare MetroRider	Optare	B25F	1990	Ex Lancaster, 1993
847	J363BNW	Optare MetroRider	Optare	B23F	1991	Ex Lancaster, 1993
850	J366BNW	Optare MetroRider	Optare	B29F	1992	Ex Lancaster, 1993

851-858
Optare MetroRider — Optare — DP28F* — 1992/3 — *855-8 are DP29F

851	K851RBB	853	K853RBB	855	L855WRG	857	L857WRG	858	L858WRG
852	K852RBB	854	K854RBB	856	L856WRG				

901-916
Freight Rover Sherpa 375 — Rootes — B16F — 1986

901	D901VCN	904	D904VCN	907	D907VCN	911	D911VCN	915	D915VCN
902	D902VCN	905	D905VCN	908	D908VCN	912	D912VCN	916	D916VCN
903	D903VCN	906	D906VCN	910	D910VCN	913	D913VCN		

Five Leyland National 2s from those originally transferred to Northumbria on its formation were the later model with Gardner LXC engines and the pod-less, light-weight body version. Now dedicated to service X2 is 784 (A133FDC) at journey's end in Newcastle. *Steve Warburton*

Four long-wheelbase Optare Metroriders have joined the Northumbria fleet for use on service 355, Newcastle to Whitley Bay. K853RBB is seen at Four Lane Ends Metro Station during May 1993. *Keith Grimes*

918-960

										Freight Rover Sherpa 374	Dormobile		DP16F*	1986-87 *933-60 are B16F

918	D918VCN	925	D925VCN	932	D932VCN	944	D944VCN	953	D953VCN
919	D919VCN	926	D926VCN	933	D933VCN	946	D946VCN	955	D955VCN
920	D920VCN	927	D927VCN	935	D935VCN	947	D947VCN	957	D957VCN
921	D921VCN	928	D928VCN	936	D936VCN	949	D949VCN	958	D958EOW
922	D922VCN	929	D929VCN	940	D940VCN	950	D950VCN	959	D959EOW
923	D923VCN	930	D930VCN	941	D941VCN	951	D951VCN	960	D960EOW
924	D924VCN	931	D931VCN	942	D942VCN	952	D952VCN		

Liveries: Grey, red and white
Blue Chip: 114
Omega Holidays: 118/20/1.
Overall advertisment: : 352/7/66, 433, 570/85 923/46.

Previous Registrations:

FSU346	B668KGX	NMS789	B336WFJ	WSV568	CUP706S
GSU346	E693JUT	OSK774	A103FPL	WSV569	CUP707S
GSU347	F570KGX	OSK775	B208NEF	WSV570	E692JUT
GSU348	F571KGX	OSU894	E113GBB	WSV571	C160UHN, NMS700
HKR11	G298SKP	OSU895	E114GBB	WSV572	B337WFJ
J20NMS	J849MCN	WLT859	D193ESC	WSV573	C139ALJ
MCU98K	JPL110K, WSV572	WSV565	ABR865S	XSV238	A141FDC
NMS100	G119UVK, WSV573	WSV566	ABR866S	YCU961T	OBR774T, WSV571
NMS700	G418WFP	WSV567	ABR867S		

Part of the National Bus intake of minibuses included a substantial number of Freight Rover Sherpas for Northumbria. While the first had bodies by Rootes the majority had Dormobile bodywork. Typical of these is 921 (D921VCN) showing the drivers sliding door, a feature of this design. *Steve Warburton*

OK TRAVEL

OK Motor Services Ltd, North Bondgate, Bishop Auckland, Co Durham, DL14 7PG

OK do not apply fleet numbers to their vehicles. However, they use the numbers of the vehicle index marks to identify the fleet and try, where possible, to obtain marks in a manner which allows this to continue. The fleet has been laid out in the sequence below, therefore, rather than by vehicle age.

Depots: North Bondgate, Bishop Auckland; Evenwood; Team Valley, Gateshead; Hunter Road, Peterlee; St Helen's Auckland (Central Works).

	Leyland Tiger TRCTL11/2R	Plaxton Supreme V Express C53F		1982-83	
LFT1X	LFT4X	XEF7Y		XEF9Y	XEF11Y
LFT2X	LFT5X	XEF8Y		XEF10Y	XEF12Y
LFT3X					

DDM20X	Leyland Leopard PSU3F/4R	Willowbrook 003	C49F	1981	Ex Crosville Wales, 1987
DDM21X	Leyland Leopard PSU3F/4R	Willowbrook 003	C49F	1981	Ex Crosville Wales, 1987
DDM25X	Leyland Leopard PSU3F/4R	Willowbrook 003	C49F	1982	Ex Crosville Wales, 1987
DDM27X	Leyland Leopard PSU3F/4R	Willowbrook 003	C49F	1982	Ex Crosville Wales, 1987
DDM28X	Leyland Leopard PSU3F/4R	Willowbrook 003	C49F	1982	Ex Crosville Wales, 1987
DDM34X	Leyland Leopard PSU3F/4R	Willowbrook 003	C49F	1982	Ex Crosville Wales, 1987
HNB35N	Leyland Atlantean AN68/1R	Northern Counties	H43/32F	1975	Ex Hunters, Seaton Delaval, 1991
HVN39V	Leyland Atlantean AN68A/1R	Alexander AL	H45/33F	1980	Ex South Yorkshire's Transport, 1991
UPT50K	Leyland Leopard PSU3D/4R	Alexander AY	B53F	1977	Ex Western Scottish, 1993
OJD53R	Bristol LH6L	Eastern Coach Works	B39F	1977	Ex Tyne & Wear Omnibus, 1990
OJD55R	Bristol LH6L	Eastern Coach Works	B39F	1976	Ex Tyne & Wear Omnibus, 1990
OJD62R	Bristol LH6L	Eastern Coach Works	B39F	1977	Ex London Transport, 1981

OK Travel had two batches of six Leyland Tigers with Plaxton Supreme V bodywork. Eleven now remain, the twelfth suffered fire damage and was rebodied with a Duple 320 body. LFT5X is seen on its way to Stockton.
Steve Warburton

	G66DHN	Iveco Daily 49-10	Phoenix	B23F	1990	
	YBO67T	Leyland Leopard PSU4E/2R	East Lancashire	B45F	1979	Ex Inter Valley Link, 1989
	YBO68T	Leyland Leopard PSU4E/2R	East Lancashire	B45F	1979	Ex Inter Valley Link, 1989
	TSJ69S	Leyland Leopard PSU3D/4R	Alexander AY	B53F	1977	Ex Western Scottish, 1993
	VFA71X	Leyland Leopard PSU3F/4R	Willowbrook 003	C49F	1982	Ex Dunn Line, Codnor, 1987
	HVN73V	Leyland Atlantean AN68A/1R	Alexander AL	H45/33F	1980	Ex South Yorkshire's Transport, 1991
	OJD76R	Bristol LH6L	Eastern Coach Works	B45F	1977	Ex Tyne & Wear Omnibus, 1990
	LBO79X	Leyland Leopard PSU3F/2R	East Lancashire	B51F	1981	Ex Inter Valley Link, 1989
	LBO80X	Leyland Leopard PSU3F/2R	East Lancashire	B51F	1981	Ex Inter Valley Link, 1989
	LBO81X	Leyland Leopard PSU4F/2R	East Lancashire	B45F	1981	Ex Inter Valley Link, 1989
	LBO82X	Leyland Leopard PSU4F/2R	East Lancashire	B45F	1981	Ex Inter Valley Link, 1989
	LBO83X	Leyland Leopard PSU4F/2R	East Lancashire	B45F	1981	Ex Inter Valley Link, 1989
	PWO87Y	Leyland Leopard PSU4G/2R	East Lancashire	B45F	1982	Ex Inter Valley Link, 1989
	PWO88Y	Leyland Leopard PSU4G/2R	East Lancashire	B45F	1982	Ex Inter Valley Link, 1989
	PWO89Y	Leyland Leopard PSU3G/2R	East Lancashire	B51F	1983	Ex Inter Valley Link, 1989
	PWO90Y	Leyland Leopard PSU3G/2R	East Lancashire	B51F	1983	Ex Inter Valley Link, 1989
	PWO91Y	Leyland Leopard PSU3G/2R	East Lancashire	B51F	1983	Ex Inter Valley Link, 1989
	OJD93R	Bristol LH6L	Eastern Coach Works	B39F	1977	Ex London Transport, 1981
	GGR103N	Leyland Atlantean AN68/2R	Northern Counties	H47/36F	1974	
w	F105UEF	Leyland Olympian ONCL10/2R	Northern Counties Palatine	H47/35F	1989	
	F106UEF	Leyland Olympian ONCL10/2R	Northern Counties Palatine	H47/35F	1989	
	F107UEF	Leyland Olympian ONCL10/2R	Northern Counties Palatine	H47/35F	1989	
	K108YVN	Leyland Olympian ON2R56C16Z4	Northern Counties Palatine	H47/35F	1992	
	K109YVN	Leyland Olympian ON2R56C16Z4	Northern Counties Palatine	H47/35F	1992	
	K110YVN	Leyland Olympian ON2R56C16Z4	Northern Counties Palatine	H47/35F	1992	
	WCK130V	Leyland Leopard PSU3E/4R	Duple Dominant II	B51F	1979	Ex Target Travel, Cramlington, 1991
	OVK136M	Leyland Atlantean AN68/1R	Alexander AL	H45/31F	1973	Ex Tyne & Wear PTE, 1983
	OVK138M	Leyland Atlantean AN68/1R	Alexander AL	H45/31F	1973	Ex Tyne & Wear PTE, 1983
	OVK148M	Leyland Atlantean AN68/1R	Alexander AL	H45/31F	1973	Ex Tyne & Wear PTE, 1983
	OVK149M	Leyland Atlantean AN68/1R	Alexander AL	H45/31F	1973	Ex Tyne & Wear PTE, 1983

	Volvo B6		Plaxton Pointer	B40F	1993
L401FVN	L404FVN	L407	L409	L411
L402FVN	L405	L408	L410	L412
L403FVN	L406			

The pride of the bus fleet are the three Northern Counties-bodied Leyland Olympians delivered in 1992. Their normal haunt is the long-established route from Bishop Auckland to Newcastle, now number 724. K109YVN is seen during June 1993 arriving at Bishop Auckland bus station. *John Carter*

APT155L	Leyland Leopard PSU3B/4R	Duple Dominant	C53F	1973	
APT156L	Leyland Leopard PSU3B/4R	Duple Dominant	C53F	1973	
APT157L	Leyland Leopard PSU3B/4R	Duple Dominant	DP53F	1973	Ex E Howe, Spennymoor, 1979
OVK164M	Leyland Atlantean AN68/1R	Alexander AL	H45/31F	1973	Ex Tyne & Wear PTE, 1983
VFT187T	Leyland Atlantean AN68/2R	MCW	H49/37F	1979	Ex Rodham, Washington, 1992
VFT188T	Leyland Atlantean AN68/2R	MCW	H49/37F	1979	Ex Go-Ahead Northern, 1992
VFT199T	Leyland Atlantean AN68/2R	MCW	H49/37F	1979	Ex Tyneside Omnibus, 1992
J201VHN	DAF SB220LC550	Optare Delta	B51F	1992	
VTY202T	Leyland Leopard PSU3/3R	Plaxton Supreme IV(1979)	C53F	1964	Ex Corse, Amble, 1979
J202VHN	DAF SB220LC550	Optare Delta	B51F	1992	
J203VHN	DAF SB220LC550	Optare Delta	B51F	1992	
J204VHN	DAF SB220LC550	Optare Delta	B51F	1992	
J205VHN	DAF SB220LC550	Optare Delta	B51F	1992	
J206VHN	DAF SB220LC550	Optare Delta	B51F	1992	
J207VHN	DAF SB220LC550	Optare Delta	B51F	1992	
YNL219V	Leyland Atlantean AN68A/2R	MCW	H49/37F	1979	Ex Go-Ahead Northern, 1991
YNL228V	Leyland Atlantean AN68A/2R	MCW	H49/37F	1979	Ex Go-Ahead Northern, 1992
YNL232V	Leyland Atlantean AN68A/2R	MCW	H49/37F	1979	Ex Hunter, Seaton Delaval, 1993
HGG245N	Leyland Atlantean AN68/1R	Alexander AL	H45/31F	1975	Ex Lonsdale, Heysham, 1986
HGG246N	Leyland Atlantean AN68/1R	Alexander AL	H45/31F	1975	Ex Lonsdale, Heysham, 1986
LBF248P	Leyland Leopard PSU3C/4R	Duple Dominant	C53F	1975	Ex Homer, Upton Warren, 1989
JPY249N	Leyland Atlantean AN68/1R	Northern Counties	H43/32F	1974	Ex Greater Manchester, 1986
JPY264N	Leyland Atlantean AN68/1R	Northern Counties	H43/32F	1974	Ex Greater Manchester, 1986
GMS278S	Leyland Leopard PSU3E/4R	Alexander AY	B53F	1978	Ex Kelvin Scottish, 1987
GMS279S	Leyland Leopard PSU3E/4R	Alexander AY	B53F	1978	Ex Midland Bluebird, 1993
GNC290N	Leyland Atlantean AN68/1R	Northern Counties	H43/32F	1975	Ex Greater Manchester, 1986
GMS291S	Leyland Leopard PSU3E/4R	Alexander AY	B53F	1978	Ex Kelvin Scottish, 1987
RUP292M	Leyland Leopard PSU3B/4R	Duple Dominant	C49F	1974	
TAJ295R	Bristol LH6L	Eastern Coach Works	B45F	1977	Ex Tyne & Wear Omnibus, 1990
WBR301R	Leyland Leopard PSU3E/4R	Plaxton Supreme III Express	C53F	1977	

OK took delivery of seven Optare Deltas in 1992 to replace six that had been leased from the suppliers. J206VHN is seen during June 1993 at Houghton Church operating one of the frequent services out of Sunderland that had commenced as soon as the 1985 Transport Act and deregulation, became effective. *David Little*

Older double deckers in the OK fleet are represented by HGG245N. This Leyland Atlantean AN68 with an Alexander body was new to Greater Glasgow PTE in the interim period between Glasgow Corporation and Strathclyde PTE. Bishop Auckland bus station is the setting for this vehicle as it operates the Witton Park service. *Steve Warburton*

To avoid a clash of numbers with Tiger PWO88Y, Bristol LH OJD88R was re-registered OJD93R while that vehicle was allocated TAJ295R by The Department of Transport. TAJ295R shows evidence of its Hillingdon ownership in the painted over offside destination box as it enters Bishop Auckland bus station. *John Carter*

Reg	Chassis	Body	Layout	Year	Notes
	Volvo B6	Plaxton Pointer	B40F	1993	

L401	L404	L407	L409	L411
L402	L405	L408	L410	L412
L403	L406			

Reg	Chassis	Body	Layout	Year	Notes
GMS306S	Leyland Leopard PSU3E/4R	Alexander AY	B53F	1978	Ex Midland Bluebird, 1993
GMS310S	Leyland Leopard PSU3E/4R	Alexander AY	B53F	1978	Ex Kelvin Scottish, 1987
ULS329T	Leyland Leopard PSU3E/4R	Alexander AY	B53F	1979	Ex Kelvin Scottish, 1987
VPT335R	Leyland Leopard PSU3E/4R	Plaxton Supreme III Express	C53F	1977	
XUP347L	Leyland Atlantean AN68/2R	Northern Counties	H47/36F	1973	
XUP348L	Leyland Atlantean AN68/2R	Northern Counties	H47/36F	1973	
XUP349L	Leyland Atlantean AN68/2R	Northern Counties	H47/36F	1973	
373FGB	Leyland Leopard PSU3E/4R	Plaxton Supreme IV	C53F	1979	Ex Frames Rickards, London, 1985
387FYM	Bristol LHS6L	Plaxton Supreme III	C33F	1978	Ex Grayline, Bicester, 1987
VUP410R	Leyland Leopard PSU3E/4R	Plaxton Supreme III	C53F	1977	
NWO446R	Leyland Leopard PSU3C/4R	Duple Dominant I	DP51F	1976	Ex National Welsh, 1989
NWO447R	Leyland Leopard PSU3C/4R	Duple Dominant I	DP51F	1976	Ex National Welsh, 1989
NWO448R	Leyland Leopard PSU3C/4R	Duple Dominant I	DP51F	1976	Ex National Welsh, 1989
NWO449R	Leyland Leopard PSU3C/4R	Duple Dominant I	C49F	1976	Ex National Welsh, 1989
NWO450R	Leyland Leopard PSU3D/4R	Duple Dominant I	DP51F	1977	Ex National Welsh, 1989
NWO451R	Leyland Leopard PSU3D/4R	Duple Dominant I	DP51F	1977	Ex National Welsh, 1989
E485ONX	Iveco Daily 49.10	Carlyle Dailybus 2	B21F	1987	Ex Carlyle, Birmingham, 1988
WGR510R	Leyland Leopard PSU3E/4R	Plaxton Supreme III Express	C53F	1977	
GBB520K	Leyland Atlantean PDR2/1	Alexander J	H48/35F	1972	Ex Tyne & Wear PTE, 1980
GBB525K	Leyland Atlantean PDR2/1	Alexander J	H48/35F	1972	Ex Tyne & Wear PTE, 1980
527LPF	Volvo B10M-61	Van Hool Alizée	C49FT	1987	Ex Kenzie, Shepreth, 1993
GBB531K	Leyland Atlantean PDR2/1	Alexander J	H48/35F	1972	Ex Tyne & Wear PTE, 1980
GBB532K	Leyland Atlantean PDR2/1	Alexander J	H48/35F	1972	Ex Tyne & Wear PTE, 1980
UBR547V	Leyland Leopard PSU3E/4R	Duple Dominant II	C53F	1979	Ex Lockey, W Auckland, 1985
NUP565M	Leyland Leopard PSU3B/4R	Duple Dominant	C53F	1973	Ex Lockey, W Auckland, 1985
LGR566P	Leyland Leopard PSU5A/4R	Plaxton Elite III Express	C57F	1975	Ex E Howe, Spennymoor, 1979
LGR567P	Leyland Leopard PSU3C/4R	Plaxton Elite III Express	C53F	1975	
LGR568P	Leyland Leopard PSU3C/4R	Plaxton Elite III Express	C53F	1975	
NNL579M	Leyland Leopard PSU3B/4R	Plaxton Elite III Express	C53F	1973	Ex Hunter, Seaton Delaval, 1988
F601TAJ	Mercedes-Benz 811D	Optare StarRider	DP29F	1988	

The first Optare vehicle to join the OK Travel fleet was StarRider F601TAJ. It was photographed at Bishop Auckland bus station on the Etherley Dene town service which is its normal route. *Steve Warburton*

LSK607	Bova FHD12.280	Bova Futura	C49FT	1985	Ex Glen, Wigginton, 1992
OSJ621R	Leyland Leopard PSU3/3R	Alexander AY	B53F	1976	Ex United, 1991
F634UEF	Iveco Daily 49.10	Carlyle Dailybus 2	B23F	1989	Ex Busways, 1992
F652KNL	Iveco Daily 49.10	Carlyle Dailybus 2	B23F	1989	Ex Busways, 1992
F656KNL	Iveco Daily 49.10	Carlyle Dailybus 2	B23F	1989	Ex Busways, 1992
F657KNL	Iveco Daily 49.10	Carlyle Dailybus 2	B23F	1989	Ex Busways, 1992
F660KNL	Iveco Daily 49.10	Carlyle Dailybus 2	B23F	1989	Ex Busways, 1992
D661CVN	Iveco Daily 49.10	Robin Hood City Nippy	B21F	1986	Ex United, 1988
D662CVN	Iveco Daily 49.10	Robin Hood City Nippy	B21F	1986	Ex United, 1988
F664VDC	Iveco Daily 49.10	Robin Hood City Nippy	B25F	1989	
G665DHN	Iveco Daily 49.10	Phoenix	B23F	1990	
G667FAJ	Iveco Daily 49.10	Phoenix	B25F	1990	
G668FAJ	Iveco Daily 49.10	Phoenix	B25F	1990	
G669FAJ	Iveco Daily 49.10	Phoenix	B25F	1990	
G670FAJ	Iveco Daily 49.10	Phoenix	B25F	1990	
HGR673N	Leyland Leopard PSU5/4R	Plaxton Elite III Express	C57F	1975	Ex E Howe, Spennymoor, 1979
CWG682V	Leyland Atlantean AN68A/1R	Alexander AL	H45/33F	1979	Ex Mainline, 1991
CWG685V	Leyland Atlantean AN68A/1R	Alexander AL	H45/33F	1979	Ex Mainline, 1991
685XHY	Bova FHD12.280	Bova Futura	C49FT	1984	Ex Goodwin, Stockport, 1991
PUP693M	Leyland Leopard PSU3B/4R	Duple Dominant	DP51F	1974	Ex Lockey, W Auckland, 1985
G701AEF	DAF MB230LB615	Duple 320	C53F	1989	
G702AEF	DAF MB230LB615	Duple 320	C53F	1989	
G703AEF	DAF MB230LB615	Duple 320	C53F	1989	
G704AEF	DAF MB230LB615	Duple 320	C53F	1989	
CWG709V	Leyland Atlantean AN68A/1R	Alexander AL	H45/33F	1980	Ex South Yorkshire's Transport, 1991
EGR710S	Leyland Leopard PSU3E/4R	Plaxton Supreme III Express	C53F	1978	
CWG714V	Leyland Atlantean AN68A/1R	Alexander AL	H45/33F	1980	Ex South Yorkshire's Transport, 1991
CWG715V	Leyland Atlantean AN68A/1R	Alexander AL	H45/33F	1980	Ex South Yorkshire's Transport, 1991
CWG717V	Leyland Atlantean AN68A/1R	Alexander AL	H45/33F	1980	Ex South Yorkshire's Transport, 1991
CWG721V	Leyland Atlantean AN68A/1R	Alexander AL	H45/33F	1980	Ex South Yorkshire's Transport, 1991
Q723GHG	Leyland Tiger TRCTL11/2R	Eastern Coach Works	B??F	1985	Ex Leyland Motors Sports Club, 1993
PKG723R	Leyland Leopard PSU3E/4RT	Duple Dominant I	DP51F	1977	Ex National Welsh, 1989
PKG724R	Leyland Leopard PSU3E/4RT	Duple Dominant I	DP51F	1977	Ex National Welsh, 1989
PKG725R	Leyland Leopard PSU3E/4RT	Duple Dominant I	DP51F	1977	Ex National Welsh, 1989
CWG728V	Leyland Atlantean AN68A/1R	Alexander AL	H45/33F	1980	Ex South Yorkshire's Transport, 1991
CWG729V	Leyland Atlantean AN68A/1R	Alexander AL	H45/33F	1980	Ex South Yorkshire's Transport, 1991
CWG730V	Leyland Atlantean AN68A/1R	Alexander AL	H45/33F	1980	Ex South Yorkshire's Transport, 1991
E734WEC	Iveco Daily 49.10	Carlyle Dailybus 2	B21F	1987	Ex Carlyle, Birmingham, 1987
UGD735	Leyland Atlantean AN68B/1R	Alexander AL	H45/33F	1981	Ex South Yorkshire's Transport, 1991
F770DWR	Bova FHD12.290	Bova Futura	C49FT	1989	Ex Palmer, Normanton, 1993
782UJO	Leyland Tiger TRCTL11/2R	Plaxton Paramount 3200	C53F	1983	Ex Stevensons, 1989
VSM783V	Leyland Leopard PSU3E/4R	Duple Dominant II	C53F	1980	Ex Lockey, W Auckland, 1985
F802UEF	DAF SB3000DKV601	Van Hool Alizée	C49FT	1989	
F803UEF	DAF SB3000DKV601	Van Hool Alizée	C49FT	1989	
J804TAJ	DAF SB3000DKV601	Van Hool Alizée	C49FT	1991	
K805BHN	DAF SB3000DKV601	Van Hool Alizée	C49FT	1993	
RNG822W	Leyland Leopard PSU3F/4R	Duple Dominant IV	C53F	1981	Ex Fishwick, Carlton Husthwaite, 1992
RNG823W	Leyland Leopard PSU3F/4R	Duple Dominant IV	C53F	1981	Ex Fishwick, Carlton Husthwaite, 1992
RNG824W	Leyland Leopard PSU3F/4R	Duple Dominant IV	C53F	1981	Ex Fishwick, Carlton Husthwaite, 1992
RNG825W	Leyland Leopard PSU3F/4R	Duple Dominant IV	C53F	1981	Ex Fishwick, Carlton Husthwaite, 1992
KBH845V	Leyland Leopard PSU3E/4R	Plaxton Supreme IV	C53F	1980	Ex Frames-Rickards, London, 1985
MBR852T	Leyland Leopard PSU3E/4R	Duple Dominant II	C53F	1979	
HEN868N	Leyland Leopard PSU4C/4R	Northern Counties	B45F	1975	Ex Halton, 1987
YSU874	Leyland Leopard PSU4E/4R	Duple Dominant I	C34F	1977	Ex National Welsh, 1989
YSU875	Leyland Leopard PSU4E/4R	Duple Dominant I	C34F	1977	Ex National Welsh, 1989
YSU876	DAF MB230LB615	Duple 320	C53F	1988	
YSU882	DAF MB230LB615	Duple 320	C53F	1988	
SKG886S	Leyland Leopard PSU3E/4R	Duple Dominant I	DP51F	1977	Ex National Welsh, 1989
SKG887S	Leyland Leopard PSU3E/4R	Duple Dominant I	C49F	1977	Ex National Welsh, 1989
SKG888S	Leyland Leopard PSU3E/4R	Duple Dominant I	C49F	1977	Ex National Welsh, 1989
SKG889S	Leyland Leopard PSU3E/4R	Duple Dominant I	C49F	1977	Ex National Welsh, 1989
D901EAJ	DAF MB230DKFL615	Duple 320	C57F	1987	
D902EAJ	DAF MB230DKFL615	Duple 320	C57F	1987	
D903EAJ	DAF MB230DKFL615	Duple 320	C57F	1987	
D904EAJ	DAF MB230DKFL615	Duple 320	C57F	1987	
D905EAJ	DAF MB230DKFL615	Duple 320	C57F	1987	
E907MDC	DAF MB230LB615	Duple 320	C57F	1988	
E908MDC	DAF MB230LB615	Duple 320	C57F	1988	
E910MDC	DAF MB230LB615	Duple 320	C57F	1988	
ESK912	Leyland Leopard PSU3B/4R	Duple Dominant	C49F	1974	Ex Hunter, Seaton Delaval, 1990
JDK923P	Leyland Leopard PSU4C/4R	Plaxton Derwent	B44F	1975	Ex Greater Manchester, 1986
MCL930P	Leyland Leopard PSU3C/4R	Alexander T	DP49F	1976	Ex Ambassador, 1987
MCL931P	Leyland Leopard PSU3C/4R	Alexander T	DP49F	1976	Ex Ambassador, 1987

During 1991 OK Travel purchased no fewer than 13 Leyland Atlantean/Alexander from South Yorkshire's Transport. Most are allocated to Team Valley depot from whence CWG709V is operating in Newcastle on local service 727 to Birtley. *Bill Potter*

A sturdy work horse in the OK fleet is Northern Counties-bodied Leyland Leopard HEN868N. The vehicle was new to Halton which, for those who still cannot get to grips with these strange names, was once Widnes. Although photographed at the Metro Centre bus station it has since been transferred to Peterlee depot. *Steve Warburton*

MCL932P	Leyland Leopard PSU3C/4R	Alexander T	DP49F	1976	Ex Ambassador, 1987
MCL933P	Leyland Leopard PSU3C/4R	Alexander T	DP49F	1976	Ex Ambassador, 1987
MCL934P	Leyland Leopard PSU3C/4R	Alexander T	DP49F	1976	Ex Ambassador, 1987
MCL935P	Leyland Leopard PSU3C/4R	Alexander T	DP49F	1976	Ex Ambassador, 1987
MCL936P	Leyland Leopard PSU3C/4R	Alexander T	DP49F	1976	Ex Ambassador, 1987
GLS950V	Leyland Leopard PSU3F/4R	Duple Dominant II	C49F	1980	Ex Kelvin Scottish, 1987
PGR961T	Leyland Leopard PSU3E/4R	Plaxton Supreme IV Express	C53F	1979	
SPT962V	Leyland Leopard PSU3E/4R	Plaxton Supreme IV Express	C53F	1980	
SPT963V	Leyland Leopard PSU3E/4R	Plaxton Supreme IV Express	C53F	1980	
SPT964V	Leyland Leopard PSU3E/4R	Plaxton Supreme IV Express	C53F	1980	
SPT965V	Volvo B58-56	Plaxton Supreme IV Express	C53F	1979	Ex Cheesey, Meadowfield, 1991
ESK982	Leyland Leopard PSU3E/4R	Duple Dominant II	C51F	1981	Ex Brighton, 1992
JIJ3737	Leyland Tiger TRCTL11/2R	Duple 320(1987)	C53F	1982	

Previous Registrations:

373FGB	KBH844V	JPY249N	GNC290N
387FYM	TOU636T	JPY264N	GNC292N, 685XHY
527LPF	D29BEW	LSK607	B113MNP, HYY3, B876HWP
685XHY	3 TRB, RJU130Y, A504KFP	OJD93R	OJD88R
782UJO	CBF2Y	TAJ295R	OJD93R
E734WEC	E961SVP	UGD735	JKW279W
ESK912	YHG3N	UPT50K	TSJ68S
ESK982	BTE207V	VSM783V	XPT566V
F634UEF	F662KNL	VTY202T	TCK722
GNC290N	HNB34N	YSU874	PKG726R
HVN39V	CWG723V	YSU875	PKG727R
HVN73V	CWG724V	YSU876	E906MDC
JIJ3737	LFT6X	YSU882	E909MDC

Liveries: Red, maroon and cream
Overall advertisements: J804TAJ, F802/3UEF

D901EAJ is the first of two batches of mid-engined DAF MB230 with Duple 320 coach bodies. It was seen near Gallowgate coach station operating an express service to Murton that runs via the Metro Centre. *Steve Warburton*

PRIMROSE COACHES

R & M Bisset Ltd, Primrose House, Holborn Gardens, Ryton, Tyne & Wear, NE40 3DN

UNL448Y	Leyland Tiger TRCTL11/3R	Duple Laser	C55F	1983	
A216BJR	Leyland Tiger TRCTL11/3R	Duple Laser	C53F	1984	
B251JNL	Leyland Tiger TRCTL11/3RH	Duple Laser 2	C53FT	1985	
B252JNL	Leyland Tiger TRCTL11/3RH	Duple Laser 2	C53FT	1985	
XFM225	Leyland Tiger TRCTL11/3RH	Duple 340	C49F	1986	Ex Crosville Wales, 1988
D224JBB	Leyland Tiger TRCTL11/3RH	Duple 340	C53F	1987	
E712FTY	Leyland Tiger TRCTL11/3ARZA	Duple 340	C53F	1988	
G141NPT	Leyland Tiger TRCTL11/3ARZA	Duple 340	C53FT	1989	
H912EFT	Volvo B10M-60	Van Hool Alizée	C53F	1991	
K919UBB	Volvo B10M-60	Jonckheere Deauville P599	C53FT	1993	

Livery: Primrose yellow and red.

Previous Registrations:
XFM225   C74KLG

Apart from the two newest coaches, all vehicles in the Primrose Coaches fleet are Leyland Tigers with Duple bodywork.
B251JNL has Duple Laser 2 bodywork and is at the coach park at Beamish Museum. Production of the Laser only
lasted from 1982 to 1985 being replaced by the 320 model for a further four years until Duple closed. *David Little*

R & M

Rochester & Marshall Ltd, Burn Lane, Hexham, Northumbria, NE46 3HN

Rochester & Marshall Ltd is a subsidiary of the Proudmutual Group.

26	HIL7596	Dennis Javelin 11SDL1905	Duple 320	C53F	1988	Ex Jason, St Mary Cray, 1993
27	GIL8487	Dennis Javelin 11SDL1905	Duple 320	C53F	1988	Ex Jason, St Mary Cray, 1993
28	IIL4579	Dennis Javelin 11SDL1905	Duple 320	C53F	1988	Ex Jason, St Mary Cray, 1993
29	IIL4580	Dennis Javelin 11SDL1905	Duple 320	C53F	1988	Ex Jason, St Mary Cray, 1993
30	GIL8488	Dennis Javelin 11SDL1905	Duple 320	C53F	1988	Ex Jason, St Mary Cray, 1993
40	WCK134V	Leyland Leopard PSU3E/4R	Duple Dominant II Express	C49F	1979	Ex Moor-Dale, Newcastle, 1993
41	WCK138V	Leyland Leopard PSU3E/4R	Duple Dominant II Express	C49F	1979	Ex Moor-Dale, Newcastle, 1993
43	MNX305	Leyland Leopard PSU3F/5R	Plaxton Supreme V	C53F	1982	Ex Curtis, Dudley, 1990
44	ONL31X	Leyland Leopard PSU3F/5R	Plaxton Supreme VI	C53F	1982	Ex Moor-Dale, Newcastle, 1990
51	OCN897R	Bedford YLQ	Plaxton Supreme III Express	C45F	1977	
53	UFT927T	Bedford YMT	Plaxton Supreme IV Express	C53F	1979	
54	BBB543V	Bedford YMT	Plaxton Supreme IV	C53F	1980	Ex Moor-Dale, Newcastle, 1984
55	BBB548V	Bedford YLQ	Plaxton Supreme IV Express	C45F	1980	
56	BBB549V	Bedford YMT	Plaxton Supreme IV Express	C53F	1980	
60	SPW101R	Leyland Leopard PSU3E/4R	Duple Dominant	B46F	1977	Ex Ambassador Travel, 1986
61	WCK131V	Leyland Leopard PSU3E/4R	Duple Dominant II Express	C49F	1979	Ex Moor-Dale, Newcastle, 1983
82	JPL168K	Leyland Atlantean PDR1A/1Sp	Park Royal	H43/29D	1972	Ex Kentish Bus, 1992
91	E676DCU	MCW MetroRider MF150	MCW	C21F	1987	Ex Moor-Dale, Newcastle, 1990

Previous Registrations:

GIL8487	E32SBO	IIL4579	E33SBO	MNX305	LTY559X
GIL8488	E38SBO	IIL4780	E37SBO	ONL31X	LTY557X, UPP938
HIL7596	E31SBO				

Bedford YMT/Duple Dominant TFT101S lays over at Gallowgate coach station, Newcastle while operating service 879 to Matfen. The arrival of the Dennis Darts with Moor-Dale has allowed Leyland Leopards to be transferred to R & M.
Steve Warburton

RAISBECK

J J Raisbeck & J R Austin, 36 Middlegate, Loansdean, Morpeth,
Northumberland NE61 2DD.

NTY906R	Bedford YLQ	Duple Dominant	C45F	1976
VRG681T	Bedford YLQ	Duple Dominant II	C45F	1978
B212JTY	Volvo B7M	East Lancashire	B53F	1985

Livery: Orange and cream

B212JTY in the Raisbeck fleet is a unique vehicle. This is the only Volvo B7M in the UK, and was one of Volvo development vehicles. Bodied by East Lancashire Coachbuilders in 1985 it was photographed while working the Bedlington town service. *David Little*

REDBY TRAVEL

Redby Travel Ltd, Hendon Road, Hendon, Sunderland, Tyne & Wear, SR2 8NT
Wearside Bus Co, Hendon Road, Hendon, Sunderland, Tyne & Wear, SR2 8NT

RYJ889R	Leyland Leopard PSU3E/4RT	Duple Dominant I	C49F	1977	Ex Brighton & Hove, 1986
OTO595R	Leyland National 11351A/1R (Volvo)		B49F	1976	Ex East Midland, 1993
RAU602R	Leyland National 11351A/1R (Volvo)		B49F	1976	Ex East Midland, 1993
MFN116R	Leyland National 11351A/1R (Volvo)		B49F	1976	Ex Robson, Thornaby, 1993
YBO331	Leyland Leopard PSU3E/4R	Willowbrook Warrior (1990)	DP48F	1980	Ex Dunstan, Moston, 1992
RSG819V	Leyland National 2 NL116L11/1R (Volvo)		B52F	1980	Ex Fife Scottish, 1993
TPC108X	Leyland Tiger TRCTL11/2R	Eastern Coach Works B51	C49F	1982	Ex Luton & District, 1991
TPC109X	Leyland Tiger TRCTL11/2R	Eastern Coach Works B51	DP49F	1982	Ex Luton & District, 1991
TPC111X	Leyland Tiger TRCTL11/2R	Eastern Coach Works B51	C49F	1982	Ex Luton & District, 1991
WPH112Y	Leyland Tiger TRCTL11/2R	Eastern Coach Works B51	C49F	1982	Ex Luton & District, 1991
WPH116Y	Leyland Tiger TRCTL11/2R	Eastern Coach Works B51	C49F	1982	Ex Luton & District, 1991
WPH119Y	Leyland Tiger TRCTL11/2R	Eastern Coach Works B51	C49F	1982	Ex Luton & District, 1991
WPH128Y	Leyland Tiger TRCTL11/2R	Eastern Coach Works B51	C49F	1982	Ex Luton & District, 1991
WPH140Y	Leyland Tiger TRCTL11/2R	Eastern Coach Works B51	C53F	1982	Ex Luton & District, 1991
WPH142Y	Leyland Tiger TRCTL11/2R	Eastern Coach Works B51	C53F	1982	Ex Luton & District, 1991
VCW598Y	Dennis Lancet SD505	Marshall Camair	B51F	1982	Ex Blackpool, 1988
SDW236Y	Dennis Lancet SD512	Wadham Stringer Vanguard	DP35F	1983	Ex Pride of the Road, Royston, 1991
A502FSS	Dennis Lancet SD516	Alexander P	B53F	1984	Ex Northern Scottish, 1991
A503FSS	Dennis Lancet SD516	Alexander P	B53F	1984	Ex Northern Scottish, 1991
A504FSS	Dennis Lancet SD516	Alexander P	B53F	1984	Ex Northern Scottish, 1991
A505FSS	Dennis Lancet SD516	Alexander P	B53F	1984	Ex Northern Scottish, 1991
B21LNR	DAF SB2300DHS585	Jonckheere Jubilee P50	C53F	1984	Ex Cochranes, Shotton, 1987
1922FS	Volvo B10M-61	Duple Laser 2	C51FT	1984	Ex Weir, Motherwell, 1985
D108XPG	Freight Rover Sherpa 374	Dormobile	B16F	1986	Ex Derby, 1992
54FS	Volvo B10M-61	Jonckheere Jubilee P50	C49FT	1986	Ex Cantabrica, Watford, 1993
55FS	Volvo B10M-61	Jonckheere Jubilee P50	C51F	1987	Ex Tellings-Golden Miller, 1990
G853UVK	Volvo B10M-60	Van Hool Alizée	C53F	1990	Ex Smith, Murton, 1992

Livery: White, fawn and green replacing red and yellow (Redby); green (Wearside buses)

Previous Registrations:

1922FS	B717MDC	54FS	C26GKX, 898CCH	55FS	D317VVV

Redby purchased four of the five Dennis Lancets from Northern Scottish in 1991. All are fitted with Alexander P-type bodywork and were initially in an all-over yellow livery. A504FSS, outside the Post Office in Kepple Street, South Shields is operating on service 556 - a route now withdrawn. *Steve Warburton*

The latest buses purchased by Redby are Leyland Nationals, the newest of which is National 2 RSG819V. This vehicle was fitted with a Volvo engine by former owner Fife Scottish. RSG819V, on one of the Sunderland town services, illustrates the full livery with fawn and green stripes. *Bill Potter*

ROBSON

G J Robson, 20 Dishforth Close, The Plantation, Thornaby-on-Tees, Cleveland, TS17 9PH

KJD421P	Bristol LH6L	Eastern Coach Works	B39F	1976	Ex Pollard, Ruan Minor, 1989
OSJ614R	Leyland Leopard PSU3C/3R	Alexander AY	B53F	1976	Ex Clydeside Scottish, 1988
C212TLY	Renault-Dodge S56	Reeve Burgess	B21F	1986	Ex Hertz, London, 1990
CBO29V	Leyland National 11351A/1R		B49F	1979	Ex National Welsh, 1990
WPH132Y	Leyland Tiger TRCTL11/2R	Eastern Coach Works	C53F	1982	Ex CharterCoach, Great Oakley, 1990
G276HDW	Freight Rover Sherpa 410	Carlyle Citybus 2	DP20F	1990	Ex National Welsh, 1992
G277HDW	Freight Rover Sherpa 410	Carlyle Citybus 2	DP20F	1990	Ex National Welsh, 1992
J485OHA	Iveco Daily 49.10	Carlyle Dailybus 2	B23F	1992	
J486OHA	Iveco Daily 49.10	Carlyle Dailybus 2	B23F	1992	

Livery: Brown and cream

On deregulation Robson of Thornaby commenced a service using two 8-seat Ford Transits. Larger capacity vehicles soon followed as evidenced by former Taff Ely Leyland National CBO29V in the familiar surroundings of Stockton High Street. *G R Mills*

ST GEORGE TRAVEL

D L Currie, St George Travel, 9 Cedar Terrace, Harraton, Washington,
Tyne & Wear, NE38 9BE

GPX587X	Mercedes-Benz L508D	Robin Hood	C19F	1981	Ex Transcity, Sidcup, 1992
G327LDT	Mercedes-Benz 609D	Whittaker	C19F	1989	
H671ATN	Toyota Coaster HB31R	Caetano Optimo	C21F	1990	

Livery: White

Despite competition from Go-Ahead Northern, the Chester-le-Street to Washington services of St George Travel survive. GPX587X, an early example of a Robin Hood conversion of the less common Mercedes-Benz L508D van (Leiferwagen) is seen during April 1993 at Washington Galleries bus station. *David Little*

SCARLET BAND

A Blenkinsop, Scarlet Band Motor Services, Welfare Garage, West Cornforth, Co Durham.

OGM605M	Leyland Leopard PSU3/3R	Alexander AYS	B53F	1974	Ex Central Scottish, 1988
PFS557M	Leyland Leopard PSU3/3R	Alexander AYS	B53F	1974	Ex Central Scottish, 1988
SCS333M	Leyland Leopard PSU3/3R	Alexander AY	B49F	1974	Ex Northern Scottish, 1988
SCS335M	Leyland Leopard PSU3/3R	Alexander AY	B49F	1974	Ex Northern Scottish, 1988
PRA13R	Leyland Leopard PSU3C/4R	Alexander T	DP53F	1976	Ex Taylor, Morley, 1992
258NOG	Van Hool T815	Van Hool Acron	C48FT	1983	
C209TLY	Renault-Dodge S56	Reeve Burgess	B21F	1986	Ex Robson, Thornaby, 1993
D684JVF	Van Hool T815	Van Hool Acron	C53FT	1987	Ex Bird, Hunstanton, 1990
E514HHN	Renault-Dodge S56	Alexander AM	B25F	1987	Ex United, 1993
E766NHN	Volvo B10M-61	Ikarus Blue Danube	C49FT	1988	
F241TBC	Volvo B10M-60	Van Hool Alizée	C51F	1989	
J200EOS	EOS E180Z	EOS 200	C53FT	1992	

Livery: Red, cream and maroon

Previous Registrations:
258NOG   From new

Scarlet Band still operate four Leyland Leopards with Alexander Y type bodies. SCS333M, with an all-alloy body of
the AY-type that features long window bays, is seen passing through North Road, Durham. *Richard Eversden*

SNAITH'S

H J Snaith, 31 Brierly Gardens, Otterburn, Northumberland

RUJ342R	Ford R1114	Plaxton Supreme III	C49F	1977	Ex Beeline, Hartlepool, 1980
WFU708V	Ford R1114	Plaxton Supreme IV	C53F	1980	Ex Zebra Holidays, Leeds, 1984
UBC644X	Ford R1114	Plaxton Supreme V	C51F	1982	Ex Allenways, Birmingham, 1985
ANA446Y	DAF MB200DKTL600	Plaxton Paramount 3200	C51F	1983	Ex Shearings, 1989
BNE69Y	Ford Transit 190	Deansgate	M12	1983	Ex Foster, Otterburn, 1992
TTY311Y	Ford Transit 190	Yeates	M12	1983	Ex Rowell, Prudhoe, 1986
A700USU	DAF MB200DKFL600	Plaxton Paramount 3200	C53F	1984	Ex Southern, Barrhead, 1991
C265GOF	Freight Rover Sherpa 350	Chassis Developments	M16	1986	
C350DND	Volvo B10M-61	Plaxton Paramount 3200 II	C53F	1986	Ex Shearings, 1993
D24SAO	Renault-Dodge S56	Reeve Burgess	B23F	1986	Ex Cumberland, 1991
D25SAO	Renault-Dodge S56	Reeve Burgess	B23F	1986	Ex Hampshire Bus, 1991
E903UBA	Freight Rover Sherpa 350	Deansgate	M16	1987	
E947TBA	Ford Transit VE6	Deansgate	M12	1987	Ex Foster, Otterburn, 1989
E852AJR	Ford Transit VE6	Snaith	M12	1987	Ex Cowie Leasing, Sunderland, 1993
E600ENL	Mercedes-Benz 609D	Devon Conversions	C21F	1988	
F568HPP	Ford Transit VE6	Chassis Developments	M16	1988	
F377ERM	Ford Transit VE6	Chassis Developments	M16	1988	Ex Brownrigg, Egremont, 1992
G400TVK	Mercedes-Benz 811D	Reeve Burgess Beaver	C25F	1989	

Livery: White, red and blue

While the majority of the vehicles operated by Snaith's of Otterburn are mini or midi buses, a number of full-size vehicles are owned including Plaxton Supreme-bodied Ford R1114, UBC644X which was photographed in Otterburn.
Bill Potter

STAR TRAVEL

Star Travel (Dipton) Ltd, 18 Poplar Grove, Dipton, Stanley, Durham, DH9 9BE

Depot: Old Colliery Yard, Tantobie

	BHN693N	Bristol RELH6L	Eastern Coach Works	DP49F	1974	Ex Catch-a-bus, East Boldon, 1991
	OBB714R	Leyland Leopard PSU3C/4R	Plaxton Supreme III Express	DP53F	1977	Ex Wansbeck, Radcliffe, 1991
	OBB715R	Leyland Leopard PSU3C/4R	Plaxton Supreme III Express	DP53F	1977	Ex Craiggs, Radcliffe, 1991
	VKH981W	Leyland Leopard PSU5D/4R	Plaxton Supreme IV	C53F	1981	Ex Scarborough & District, 1991
	XBD556W	DAF MB200DKTL600	Jonckheere Jubilee P50	C51FT	1981	Ex Anenalink, Dundee, 1989
	PNW335W	Leyland Leopard PSU5D/4R	Plaxton Supreme IV	C49F	1981	Ex Scarborough & District, 1991
	C43HDT	Dennis Domino SDA1202	Optare	B33F	1985	Ex Stevensons, 1992
	C44HDT	Dennis Domino SDA1202	Optare	B33F	1985	Ex Stevensons, 1992
u	D169LNA	Freight Rover Sherpa 350	Made-to-Measure	M16	1986	
	D350JUM	Volkswagen LT55	Optare City Pacer	B25F	1986	Ex London Buses, 1992

Livery: Two-tone blue

Previous Registrations:
VKH981W   PNW301W, YUU556

Star Travel continues to operate a number of routes out of Stanley bus station. Bristol RELH/Eastern Coach Works, BHN693N, is seen at Star Travel's depot still wearing Catch a Bus livery. This vehicle is currently out of use awaiting a decision on its future. *David Little*

TARGET COACHES

Crown Coaches (Cramlington) Ltd, Station Road, Cramlington,
Northumberland, NE23 9DL

BNB244T	Leyland Leopard PSU5C/4R	Duple Dominant II	C50F	1979	Ex Brownrigg, Egremont, 1992
XGS773X	Leyland Leopard PSU5D/4R	Plaxton Supreme IV	C50F	1981	Ex Target Travel, Cramlington, 1991
KLX108	Leyland Tiger TRCTL11/3R	Duple Caribbean	C50F	1983	Ex Dover, Hetton, 1993
E205AJR	Mercedes-Benz L307D	Reeve Burgess	M12	1987	Ex Target Taxis, Cramlington, 1992
E371JTN	Mercedes-Benz 407D	Reeve Burgess	M15	1988	Ex Target Taxis, Cramlington, 1992
G514SJR	Mercedes-Benz 408D	Devon Conversions	M15	1989	Ex Target Taxis, Cramlington, 1992
G277WFT	Mercedes-Benz L308D	Devon Conversions	M15	1989	Ex Target Taxis, Cramlington, 1992

Livery: Blue or white

Previous Registrations:
KLX108   DLJ577Y

Crown Coaches, Cramlington still trades using the Target fleetname. Vehicles are either in all-over white or in a pale blue livery. Leyland Leopard BNB244T, with a Duple Dominant body, is seen during May 1993 departing from Haymarket bus station, Newcastle. *Keith Grimes*

TRANSIT

Cleveland Transit Ltd, Church Road, Stockton-on-Tees, Cleveland, TS18 2HW
Cleveland Coaches Ltd, Church Road, Stockton-on-Tees, Cleveland, TS18 2HW

1-10			Leyland Lynx LX112L10ZR1R			Leyland Lxnx		B49F	1989		
1	F601UVN	3	F603UVN	5	F605UVN		7	F607UVN		9	F609UVN
2	F602UVN	4	F604UVN	6	F606UVN		8	F608UVN		10	F610UVN

11-20			Leyland Lynx LX2R11C15Z4R			Leyland Lynx 2		B51F	1989		
11	G611GEF	13	G613GEF	15	G615GEF		17	G617GEF		19	G619GEF
12	G612GEF	14	G614GEF	16	G616GEF		18	G618GEF		20	G620GEF

21	J901UKV	Leyland Lynx LX2R11V18Z4S		Leyland Lynx 2	B49F	1991	Ex Volvo demonstrator, 1992

22-30			Leyland Lynx LX2R11V18Z4R			Leyland Lynx 2		B49F	1992		
22	K622YVN	24	K624YVN	26	K626YVN		28	K628YVN		30	K630YVN
23	K623YVN	25	K625YVN	27	K627YVN		29	K629YVN			

31	L31	Volvo B6	Plaxton Pointer	B40F	1993
32	L32	Volvo B6	Plaxton Pointer	B40F	1993
33	L33	Volvo B6	Plaxton Pointer	B40F	1993

34-40			Volvo B10B			Plaxton Verde		B50F	1993		
34	L34	36	L36	38	L38		39	L39		40	L40
35	L35	37	L37								

Transit operate a total of 30 Leyland Lynx with both principal models being represented. Numerically last of the first delivery is 10 (F610UVN), showing the nearside arrangement of these vehicles as it travels along Stockton High Street while operating local service 51. Later deliveries include Cummins-engined and Volvo-engined examples, the latter also carrying the Lynx 2 body. *G R Mills*

121-157 — Leyland Fleetline FE30AGR — Northern Counties — H43/31F — 1978-83

121	YVN521T	**129**	GAJ129V	**137**	JAJ137W	**144**	JAJ144W	**151**	VEF151Y
122	YVN522T	**130**	GAJ130V	**138**	JAJ138W	**145**	JAJ145W	**152**	VEF152Y
123	YVN523T	**131**	GAJ131V	**139**	JAJ139W	**146**	JAJ146W	**153**	VEF153Y
124	YVN524T	**132**	GAJ132V	**140**	JAJ140W	**147**	PEF147X	**154**	YAJ154Y
125	GAJ125V	**133**	GAJ133V	**141**	JAJ141W	**148**	PEF148X	**155**	YAJ155Y
126	GAJ126V	**134**	GAJ134V	**142**	JAJ142W	**149**	PEF149X	**156**	YAJ156Y
127	GAJ127V	**135**	GAJ135V	**143**	JAJ143W	**150**	VEF150Y	**157**	YAJ157Y
128	GAJ128V	**136**	GAJ136V						

200-207 — Dennis Dominator DD149* — Northern Counties — H43/31F — 1980-84 *200/201 are DD121B

200	GAJ200V	**202**	VVN202Y	**204**	A204EHN	**206**	A206EHN	**207**	A207EHN
201	GAJ201V	**203**	VVN203Y	**205**	A205EHN				

208-213 — Dennis Dominator DDA167* — Northern Counties — H43/31F — 1980-84 *213 is DDA172

208	A208EHN	**209**	A209FHN	**211**	A211FVN	**212**	A212EHN	**213**	A213FVN

214-222 — Dennis Dominator DD906* — Northern Counties — H43/31F — 1985-86 *219-22 are DDA1009

214	B214OAJ	**216**	B216OAJ	**218**	B218OAJ	**220**	C220WAJ	**222**	C222WAJ
215	B215OAJ	**217**	B217OAJ	**219**	C219WAJ	**221**	C221WAJ		

335 — F335SPY — Renault-Dodge S56 — Northern Counties — DP21F — 1988

336-345 — Renault-Dodge S56 — Northern Counties — B23F — 1989

336	F336VEF	**338**	F338VEF	**340**	F340VEF	**342**	F342VEF	**344**	F344VEF
337	F337VEF	**339**	F339VEF	**341**	F341VEF	**343**	F343VEF	**345**	F345VEF

Transit operate numerous Leyland Fleetlines all fitted with Northern Counties bodywork. No.123 (YVN523T) has recently been refurbished and had its upper deck front windows rebuilt. It now represents the oldest batch of double deck buses remaining in service in the main fleet. *John Carter*

The Cleveland Coaches fleet comprises not only coaches used on such work but also a number of elderly double deckers used on school contracts and works services. Leyland Tiger 952 (OIB3515) was originally registered YHN452Y and was photographed at Middlesbrough bus station. *G R Mills*

Following the end of Fleetline production, Cleveland Transit turned to the Dennis Dominator for its next batches of double deckers although Northern Counties continued to be the preferred body builder. One of the penultimate batch 214 (B214OAJ) is seen at the northern end of Stockton High Street. *G R Mills*

405-419 — Leyland Leopard PSU3E/4R — Plaxton Supreme IV Express DP53F — 1979-80

405	CPY705T	411	FDC411V	414	FDC414V	416	FDC416V	418	FDC418V
409	FDC409V	412	FDC412V	415	FDC415V	417	FDC417V	419	FDC419V
410	FDC410V								

420-424 — Leyland Leopard PSU3F/4R — Plaxton Supreme IV Express DP53F* — 1980

420	FDC420V	421	HPY421V	422	HPY422V	423	HPY423V	424	HPY424V

500	PRX189B	Leyland Titan PD3/4	Northern Counties	FCO39/30F	1964	Ex Southdown, 1988

Cleveland Coaches Ltd:

900	CVN400T	Bedford YLQ/S	Duple Dominant II	C35F	1979	
902	BPY402T	Leyland Leopard PSU3E/4R	Plaxton Supreme IV Express	DP53F	1979	
903	BPY403T	Leyland Leopard PSU3E/4R	Plaxton Supreme IV Express	DP53F	1979	
920	YVN520T	Leyland Fleetline FE30AGR	Northern Counties	H43/31F	1979	
923	D323HDC	Renault-Dodge S56	Northern Counties	B20F	1987	
924	E324JVN	Renault-Dodge S56	Northern Counties	B20F	1987	
925	HPY425V	Leyland Leopard PSU3F/4R	Plaxton Supreme IV Express	DP53F	1980	
926	HPY426X	Leyland Leopard PSU3F/4R	Plaxton Supreme IV Express	DP53F	1980	
927	OHN427X	Leyland Leopard PSU3F/4R	Plaxton Supreme IV Express	C53F	1981	
928	OHN428X	Leyland Leopard PSU3F/4R	Plaxton Supreme IV Express	C53F	1981	
929	OHN429X	Leyland Leopard PSU3F/4R	Plaxton Supreme IV Express	C53F	1981	
933	E333LHN	Renault-Dodge S56	Northern Counties	DP21F	1988	
941	SDC141H	Leyland Atlantean PDR1A/1	Northern Counties (1985)	H43/31F	1970	
942	SDC142H	Leyland Atlantean PDR1A/1	Northern Counties (1985)	H43/31F	1970	
946	SDC146H	Leyland Atlantean PDR1A/1	Northern Counties (1984)	H43/31F	1970	
947	SDC147H	Leyland Atlantean PDR1A/1	Northern Counties (1983)	H43/31F	1970	
951	OIB3516	Leyland Tiger TRCTL11/2R	Plaxton Paramount 3200	C49F	1983	
952	OIB3515	Leyland Tiger TRCTL11/2R	Plaxton Paramount 3200	C49F	1983	
953	OIB3514	Leyland Tiger TRCTL11/2RP	Plaxton Paramount 3200	C49F	1984	
954	OIB3513	Leyland Tiger TRCTL11/2RP	Plaxton Paramount 3200	C49F	1984	
955	OIB3512	Leyland Royal Tiger RTC	Roe Doyen	C53F	1987	
983	PJI4983	Leyland Olympian ONTL11/2RSp	Eastern Coach Works	CH45/28F	1985	Ex Clyde Coast, Ardrossan, 1992
986	PJI4986	Volvo B10M-61	Van Hool Alizée	C49F	1988	Ex Excelsior, 1993
997	AHN397T	Leyland Leopard PSU3E/4R	Plaxton Supreme IV Express	DP55F	1979	
998	BAJ998T	Leyland Leopard PSU3E/4R	Plaxton Supreme IV Express	DP55F	1979	

Livery: Green and yellow
Overall advertisments: 1-6, 201/16.

Previous Registrations:

OIB3512	D455GHN	OIB3515	YHN452Y	PJI4986	E304OPR
OIB3513	A454HPY	OIB3516	YHN451Y	PRX189B	417DCD
OIB3514	A453HPY	PJI4983	B577LPE		

During 1992 Cleveland Coaches purchased a Leyland Olympian/Eastern Coach Works double-deck coach from Clyde Coast, Ardrossan. No.983 (PJI4983), which was new to Alder Valley as B577LPE, is seen at the Metro Centre coach park.
Phillip Stephenson

TYNE VALLEY

Tyne Valley Coaches Ltd, Acomb, Hexham, Northumberland, NE46 4QT

GAN744J	Leyland Leopard PSU5/4RT	Plaxton Elite II	C57F	1971	Ex Marshall, Blackpool, 1976
GAN745J	Leyland Leopard PSU5/4RT	Plaxton Elite II	C57F	1971	Ex Marshall, Blackpool, 1976
GJR494L	Leyland Leopard PSU3B/4R	Plaxton Elite III Express	C49F	1973	
HTY481L	Leyland Leopard PSU3B/4R	Plaxton Elite III Express	C53F	1973	
HVK185N	Leyland Leopard PSU3B/4R	Plaxton Elite III Express	C53F	1975	
HVK186N	Leyland Leopard PSU3B/4R	Plaxton Elite III Express	C53F	1975	
YSU919	Leyland Leopard PSU3C/4R	Duple Dominant	C53F	1977	
TNL628S	Leyland Leopard PSU5A/4R	Plaxton Supreme III	C57F	1978	
NSU969	Volvo B58-56	Duple Dominant II	C49F	1979	
CBB18V	Leyland Leopard PSU3E/4R	Duple Dominant II	C53F	1980	
CBB19V	Leyland Leopard PSU3E/4R	Duple Dominant II	C53F	1980	
XSV218	Leyland Leopard PSU5D/4R	Duple Dominant III	C57F	1983	
XSV220	Leyland Tiger TRCTL11/3R	Duple Laser	C53F	1984	
XSV219	Leyland Tiger TRCTL11/3R	Plaxton Paramount 3500	C53F	1985	
YSU920	Leyland Tiger TRCTL11/3RZM	Duple 320	C57F	1989	

Livery: Two-tone blue

Previous Registrations:

NSU969	XNL870T	XSV219	B969HTY	YSU919	ONL772R
XSV218	UFT252Y	XSV220	A105BUR	YSU920	F27TMP

Tyne Valley's newest coaches now all carry cherished registration marks. YSU920 is the youngest and was originally registered F27TMP by the now-defunct dealers, Arlington. This Leyland Tiger has a Duple 320 body and is seen at Tyne Valley's Acomb depot. The 320 has a larger capacity than most contemporaries of its type. It has been certified upto 61 seats, although 57 is the preferred maximum for most operators. *David Little*

UNITED/TEES/TMS

Tees & District Transport Company Ltd,
Teesside Motor Services Ltd,
United Automobile Services Ltd, United House, Grange Road, Darlington,
Co Durham, DL1 5NL

United, Tees and TMS are part of the Westcourt group and are managed by North East Bus Limited. A common fleet numbering system is used and the combined fleet is listed below.

Depots:
Tees - Church Square, Hartlepool; Whitby Road, Loftus; Union Street, Middlesbrough; Railway Terrace, Redcar; and North Road, Stokesley.
TMS - Boathouse Lane, Stockton.
United - Morland Street, Bishop Auckland; Feethams, Darlington; Waddington Street, Durham; Davey Drive, Peterlee; Station Yard, Richmond and Park Street, Ripon

206-238
Leyland Olympian ONLXB/1R   Eastern Coach Works   H45/32F*   1982-83   *233/4 are DPH40/28F

206	SPY206X	214	WDC214Y	218	WDC218Y	227	AEF227Y	235	A235GHN
207	SPY207X	215	WDC215Y	223	AEF223Y	228	AEF228Y	236	A236GHN
208	SPY208X	216	WDC216Y	225	AEF225Y	233	A233GHN	237	A237GHN
209	SPY209X	217	WDC217Y	226	AEF226Y	234	A234GHN	238	A238GHN

245	B45NDX	Leyland Olympian ONLXB/1RV	East Lancashire	H40/33F	1985	Ex Stevensons, 1993
251	B251NVN	Leyland Olympian ONLXB/1R	Eastern Coach Works	H45/32F	1984	
252	B252PHN	Leyland Olympian ONLXB/1R	Eastern Coach Works	H45/32F	1984	
253	B253PHN	Leyland Olympian ONLXB/1R	Eastern Coach Works	H45/32F	1984	
255	B255RAJ	Leyland Olympian ONLXB/1R	Eastern Coach Works	H45/32F	1984	
263	E963PME	Leyland Olympian ONLXB/1R	Optare	H47/29F	1988	Ex London Cityrama, 1992
265	C265XEF	Leyland Olympian ONLXB/1R	Eastern Coach Works	DPH42/30F	1985	
266	C266XEF	Leyland Olympian ONLXB/1R	Eastern Coach Works	DPH42/30F	1985	
267	C267XEF	Leyland Olympian ONLXB/1R	Eastern Coach Works	DPH42/30F	1985	
268	C268XEF	Leyland Olympian ONLXB/1R	Eastern Coach Works	DPH42/30F	1985	

271-275
Leyland Olympian ON2R50C13Z4 Alexander RH   H46/28F   1993

271	L271FVN	272	L272FVN	273	L273FVN	274	L274FVN	275	L275FVN

The Tyne Link branding was used on vehicles which operated on the X1 and X10 Express services between Middlesbrough and Newcastle. Tees' Leyland Olympian with standard Eastern Coach Works body, 267 (C267XEF), is seen at Scarborough about to operate service X93 to Middlesbrough.
G R Mills

United and Tees still operate a good number of Bristol VRTs and have, in recent years added examples from West Riding, Yorkshire Woollen and Trent. No.755 (DUP755S), however, was new to United as was photographed in the narrow streets of Richmond operating service 27 to Darlington. *Steve Warburton*

565	OWW905P	Bristol VRT/SL3/6LXB	Eastern Coach Works	H43/31F	1976	Ex West Riding, 1990
567	OWW907P	Bristol VRT/SL3/6LXB	Eastern Coach Works	H43/31F	1976	Ex West Riding, 1990
570	NWR505P	Bristol VRT/SL3/6LXB	Eastern Coach Works	H43/31F	1976	Ex West Riding, 1990
572	NWR507P	Bristol VRT/SL3/6LXB	Eastern Coach Works	H43/31F	1976	Ex West Riding, 1990
573	NWR508P	Bristol VRT/SL3/6LXB	Eastern Coach Works	H43/31F	1976	Ex West Riding, 1990

696-828

		Bristol VRT/SL3/6LXB	Eastern Coach Works	H43/31F*	1975-81	*814 is DPH41/29F

696	UGR696R	755	DUP755S	771	OBR771T	804	XPT804V	814	APT814W
699	UGR699R	756	DUP756S	780	SGR780V	805	XPT805V	822	MEF822W
713	AUP713S	761	HUP761T	781	SGR781V	808	APT808W	823	MEF823W
730	CPT730S	763	HUP763T	786	SGR786V	809	APT809W	824	MEF824W
744	DUP744S	765	HUP765T	794	SGR794V	812	APT812W	828	PAJ828X
751	DUP751S	770	OBR770T	801	XPT801V	813	APT813W		

831	RAU811R	Bristol VRT/SL3/501(Gardner)	Eastern Coach Works	H43/31F	1977	Ex Trent, 1992
832	URB822S	Bristol VRT/SL3/501(Gardner)	Eastern Coach Works	H43/31F	1977	Ex Trent, 1992
833	URB823S	Bristol VRT/SL3/501(Gardner)	Eastern Coach Works	H43/31F	1977	Ex Trent, 1992
834	URB824S	Bristol VRT/SL3/501(Gardner)	Eastern Coach Works	H43/31F	1977	Ex Trent, 1992
836	RYG390R	Bristol VRT/SL3/6LXB	Eastern Coach Works	H43/31F	1977	Ex West Riding, 1991
838	RYG392R	Bristol VRT/SL3/6LXB	Eastern Coach Works	H43/31F	1977	Ex West Riding, 1991
841	UNW930R	Bristol VRT/SL3/6LXB	Eastern Coach Works	H43/31F	1977	Ex West Riding, 1990
842	UNW931R	Bristol VRT/SL3/6LXB	Eastern Coach Works	H43/31F	1977	Ex West Riding, 1990
843	XWU339S	Bristol VRT/SL3/6LXB	Eastern Coach Works	H43/31F	1977	Ex West Riding, 1990
844	YNW290S	Bristol VRT/SL3/6LXB	Eastern Coach Works	H43/31F	1978	Ex West Riding, 1990
845	YNW291S	Bristol VRT/SL3/6LXB	Eastern Coach Works	H43/31F	1978	Ex West Riding, 1990
850	YNW292S	Bristol VRT/SL3/6LXB	Eastern Coach Works	H43/31F	1978	Ex West Riding, 1991
851	YNW293S	Bristol VRT/SL3/6LXB	Eastern Coach Works	H43/31F	1978	Ex West Riding, 1991
852	YNW294S	Bristol VRT/SL3/6LXB	Eastern Coach Works	H43/31F	1978	Ex West Riding, 1991
856	XNW868S	Bristol VRT/SL3/6LXB	Eastern Coach Works	H43/31F	1977	Ex West Riding, 1991
857	XNW869S	Bristol VRT/SL3/6LXB	Eastern Coach Works	H43/31F	1977	Ex West Riding, 1991
858	XNW870S	Bristol VRT/SL3/6LXB	Eastern Coach Works	H43/31F	1977	Ex West Riding, 1991
862	CWU324T	Bristol VRT/SL3/6LXB	Eastern Coach Works	H43/31F	1978	Ex West Riding, 1991

One regular route for United's Plaxton Paramount-bodied Leyland Tigers is service X14 from Bishop Auckland, via Shildon and Darlington, to Middlesbrough. United 1305 (B266 KPF) is seen during May 1993 in Tubwell Row, Darlington. *David Little.*

The Optare Vecta is constructed in Leeds and uses a MAN engine and ZF gearbox, both produced in Germany. With a maximum seating capacity of 45, it is considered an ideal successor to Bristol LH. TMS, part of the North East Bus Group was the first in the area to receive to type, and 1502 (J620UHN) was photographed in Stockton shortly after delivery. *Keith Grimes*

United 3143 (RHG882X) is a Leyland National mark 2 that has now seen service with four operators. New to Ribble in 1982 it was transferred with the northern area operation to Cumberland. In 1987 it was sold to the Shearings group at a time when that operator was expanding into stage carriage operations. It joined United in 1991 and is pictured in Darlington. *Keith Grimes*

864	CWU326T	Bristol VRT/SL3/6LXB	Eastern Coach Works	H43/31F	1978	Ex West Riding, 1991
865	CWU327T	Bristol VRT/SL3/6LXB	Eastern Coach Works	H43/31F	1978	Ex West Riding, 1991
866	DWY138T	Bristol VRT/SL3/6LXB	Eastern Coach Works	H43/31F	1978	Ex West Riding, 1991
867	DWY139T	Bristol VRT/SL3/6LXB	Eastern Coach Works	H43/31F	1978	Ex West Riding, 1991
876	DWY148T	Bristol VRT/SL3/6LXB	Eastern Coach Works	H43/31F	1979	Ex West Riding, 1991
879	JYG429V	Bristol VRT/SL3/6LXB	Eastern Coach Works	H43/31F	1979	Ex West Riding, 1991
880	JYG430V	Bristol VRT/SL3/6LXB	Eastern Coach Works	H43/31F	1979	Ex West Riding, 1991
892	PWR442W	Bristol VRT/SL3/6LXB	Eastern Coach Works	H43/31F	1980	Ex West Riding, 1992
895	PWR445W	Bristol VRT/SL3/6LXB	Eastern Coach Works	H43/31F	1980	Ex West Riding, 1992
1009	JUP109T	Leyland Leopard PSU5C/4R	Plaxton Supreme III	C50F	1978	
1011	JUP111T	Leyland Leopard PSU5C/4R	Plaxton Supreme III	C50F	1978	
1012	JUP112T	Leyland Leopard PSU5C/4R	Plaxton Supreme III	DP63F	1979	
1013	JUP113T	Leyland Leopard PSU5C/4R	Plaxton Supreme III	C50F	1979	
1022	PPT822T	Leyland Leopard PSU5C/4R	Plaxton Supreme IV	C51F	1979	
1025	SBR525V	Leyland Leopard PSU5C/4R	Plaxton Supreme IV	C51F	1979	
1042	DAK222V	Leyland Leopard PSU5C/4R	Duple Dominant II	C53F	1980	Ex Sheffield & District, 1988
1112	LGR412T	Leyland Leopard PSU3E/4R	Plaxton Supreme III Express	C49F	1978	
1119	SPT219V	Leyland Leopard PSU3E/4R	Plaxton Supreme IV Express	C49F	1979	

1210-1222		Leyland Leopard PSU3E/4R	Duple Dominant	B55F	1979-81 Ex Trimdon, 1990		
1210	MGR913T	**1212**	MGR917T	**1218**	VUP513V	**1220**	LPY457W	**1222**	LPY459W
1211	MGR915T						

1225	TDC855X	Leyland Tiger TRCTL11/2R	Duple Dominant	B55F	1982	Ex Trimdon, 1990
1226	TDC856X	Leyland Tiger TRCTL11/2R	Duple Dominant	B55F	1982	Ex Trimdon, 1990
1227	TDC857X	Leyland Tiger TRCTL11/2R	Duple Dominant	B55F	1982	Ex Trimdon, 1990
1228	B957LHN	Leyland Tiger TRBTL11/2RH	Duple Dominant	B55F	1984	Ex Trimdon, 1990
1229	B958LHN	Leyland Tiger TRBTL11/2RH	Duple Dominant	B55F	1984	Ex Trimdon, 1990
1230	B959LHN	Leyland Tiger TRBTL11/2RH	Duple Dominant	B55F	1984	Ex Trimdon, 1990
1231	C74UHN	Leyland Tiger TRCTL11/2RP	Duple Dominant	B55F	1985	Ex Trimdon, 1990
1232	C75UHN	Leyland Tiger TRCTL11/2RP	Duple Dominant	B55F	1985	Ex Trimdon, 1990
1233	C76UHN	Leyland Tiger TRCTL11/2RP	Duple Dominant	B55F	1985	Ex Trimdon, 1990
1234	H278LEF	Leyland Tiger TRCL10/3ARZA	Alexander Q	B55F	1990	
1235	H279LEF	Leyland Tiger TRCL10/3ARZA	Alexander Q	B55F	1990	
1301	A516EVN	Leyland Tiger TRCTL11/2R	Plaxton Paramount 3200 E	C47F	1983	
1302	A517EVN	Leyland Tiger TRCTL11/2R	Plaxton Paramount 3200 E	C47F	1983	
1303	A518EVN	Leyland Tiger TRCTL11/2R	Plaxton Paramount 3200 E	C47F	1983	
1304	A519EVN	Leyland Tiger TRCTL11/2R	Plaxton Paramount 3200 E	C47F	1983	
1305	B266KPF	Leyland Tiger TRCTL11/2R	Plaxton Paramount 3200 IIE	C53F	1985	Ex Green, Kirkintilloch, 1990

1306-1315

		Leyland Tiger TRCTL11/2RP	Plaxton Paramount 3200 III	C47F*	1987	*1311-15 are C53F

1306	E266KEF	1308	E268KEF	1310	E270KEF	1312	E272KEF	1314	E274KEF
1307	E267KEF	1309	E269KEF	1311	E271KEF	1313	E273KEF	1315	E275KEF

1316	EWY26Y	Leyland Tiger TRCTL11/2R	Alexander TE	C49F	1983	Ex West Riding, 1990
1317	EWY27Y	Leyland Tiger TRCTL11/2R	Alexander TE	C49F	1983	Ex West Riding, 1990
1318	EWY28Y	Leyland Tiger TRCTL11/2R	Alexander TE	C49F	1983	Ex West Riding, 1990
1319	A105EPA	Leyland Tiger TRCTL11/2R	Plaxton Paramount 3200 E	C53F	1983	Ex Regal, Kirkintilloch, 1992
1320	EWY30Y	Leyland Tiger TRCTL11/2R	Alexander TE	C49F	1983	Ex West Riding, 1990
1321	A32LWX	Leyland Tiger TRCTL11/2R	Alexander TE	C49F	1983	Ex West Riding, 1990
1322	A31LWX	Leyland Tiger TRCTL11/2R	Alexander TE	C49F	1983	Ex West Riding, 1990
1323	A33LWX	Leyland Tiger TRCTL11/2R	Alexander TE	C49F	1983	Ex West Riding, 1990
1324	C39CWT	Leyland Tiger TRCTL11/2RH	Plaxton Paramount 3200 IIE	C49F	1986	Ex West Riding, 1991
1325	C40CWT	Leyland Tiger TRCTL11/2RH	Plaxton Paramount 3200 IIE	C49F	1986	Ex West Riding, 1991
1327	NLG35Y	Leyland Tiger TRCTL11/2R	Plaxton Paramount 3200 E	C51F	1983	Ex Careline, Coventry, 1992
1328	LHO992Y	Leyland Tiger TRCTL11/2R	Plaxton Paramount 3200 E	C53F	1983	Ex Tillingbourne, 1992
1329	C36CWT	Leyland Tiger TRCTL11/2RH	Plaxton Paramount 3200 IIE	C49F	1986	Ex West Riding, 1992
1330	C37CWT	Leyland Tiger TRCTL11/2RH	Plaxton Paramount 3200 IIE	C49F	1986	Ex West Riding, 1992
1331	C38CWT	Leyland Tiger TRCTL11/2RH	Plaxton Paramount 3200 IIE	C53F	1986	Ex West Riding, 1992
1332	A116EPA	Leyland Tiger TRCTL11/2R	Plaxton Paramount 3200 E	C53F	1983	Ex London & Country, 1992
1333	A117EPA	Leyland Tiger TRCTL11/2R	Plaxton Paramount 3200 E	C53F	1983	Ex London & Country, 1992
1334	A119EPA	Leyland Tiger TRCTL11/2R	Plaxton Paramount 3200 E	C53F	1983	Ex London & Country, 1992
1335	A120EPA	Leyland Tiger TRCTL11/2R	Plaxton Paramount 3200 E	C53F	1983	Ex London & Country, 1992
1336	A122EPA	Leyland Tiger TRCTL11/2R	Plaxton Paramount 3200 E	C53F	1984	Ex London & Country, 1992
1337	A132EPA	Leyland Tiger TRCTL11/2R	Plaxton Paramount 3200 E	C49F	1984	Ex London & Country, 1992
1338	REP328Y	Leyland Tiger TRCTL11/2R	Plaxton Paramount 3200 E	C53F	1983	Ex Chisholm, Ramsgate, 1993
1339	RMO202Y	Leyland Tiger TRCTL11/2R	Plaxton Paramount 3200 E	C53F	1983	Ex Pulham, Bourton, 1993
1340	RMO204Y	Leyland Tiger TRCTL11/2R	Plaxton Paramount 3200 E	C53F	1983	Ex Pulham, Bourton, 1993
1341	RMO201Y	Leyland Tiger TRCTL11/2R	Plaxton Paramount 3200 E	C53F	1983	Ex Pulham, Bourton, 1993

1342-1346

		Leyland Tiger TRCTL11/2R	Plaxton Paramount 3200 IIE	C49F	1986	Ex West Riding, 1993

1342	C42CWT	1343	C43CWT	1344	C34CWT	1345	C35CWT	1346	C41CWT

A considerable number of Leyland Tigers, mostly with Plaxton Paramount bodies, have been acquired by the Westcourt group or its predecessor Caldaire North-East for use on the longer stage services. No.1329 (C36CWT) is seen at Loftus on service 850 to Whitby. *G R Mills*

1401	C131HJN	Leyland Tiger TRCTL11/3RH	Plaxton Paramount 3200 II	C53F	1983	Ex Eastern National, 1989
1402	C132HJN	Leyland Tiger TRCTL11/3RH	Plaxton Paramount 3200 II	C53F	1983	Ex Eastern National, 1989
1403	C133HJN	Leyland Tiger TRCTL11/3RH	Plaxton Paramount 3200 II	C53F	1983	Ex Eastern National, 1989
1404	B112GRR	Leyland Tiger TRCTL11/3RH	Plaxton Paramount 3200 II	C51F	1985	Ex Trent, 1991
1405	B113GRR	Leyland Tiger TRCTL11/3RH	Plaxton Paramount 3200 II	C51F	1985	Ex Trent, 1991
1406	A949KAJ	Leyland Tiger TRCTL11/3R	Plaxton Paramount 3200 E	C57F	1983	Ex Vanguard, Bedworth, 1991
1407	EAH891Y	Leyland Tiger TRCTL11/3R	Plaxton Paramount 3200 E	DP61F	1983	Ex Green, Kirkintilloch, 1991
1408	EAH888Y	Leyland Tiger TRCTL11/3R	Plaxton Paramount 3200 E	C53F	1983	Ex Green, Kirkintilloch, 1991
1409	A98OVF	Leyland Tiger TRCTL11/3R	Plaxton Paramount 3200 E	C53F	1983	Ex Ambassador Travel, 1991
1410	B110GRR	Leyland Tiger TRCTL11/3R	Plaxton Paramount 3200 II	C51F	1985	Ex Trent, 1991
1411	B906RVF	Leyland Tiger TRCTL11/3RH	Plaxton Paramount 3200 IIE	C53F	1985	Ex Ambassador Travel, 1991
1412	B907RVF	Leyland Tiger TRCTL11/3RH	Plaxton Paramount 3200 IIE	C53F	1985	Ex Ambassador Travel, 1991
1413	ERF23Y	Leyland Tiger TRCTL11/3R	Plaxton Paramount 3200 E	C53F	1983	Ex Bell, Sunderland, 1991
1414	EAH887Y	Leyland Tiger TRCTL11/3R	Plaxton Paramount 3200 E	DP61F	1983	Ex Ambassador Travel, 1991
1415	B111GRR	Leyland Tiger TRCTL11/3RH	Plaxton Paramount 3200 II	C51F	1985	Ex Trent, 1991
1416	B114GRR	Leyland Tiger TRCTL11/3R	Plaxton Paramount 3200 II	C51F	1985	Ex Trent, 1991
1417	B115GRR	Leyland Tiger TRCTL11/3RH	Plaxton Paramount 3200 II	C51F	1985	Ex Trent, 1991
1418	B908RVF	Leyland Tiger TRCTL11/3R	Plaxton Paramount 3200 IIE	C53F	1985	Ex Ambassador Travel, 1991
1419	A146EPA	Leyland Tiger TRCTL11/3R	Plaxton Paramount 3200 E	DP61F	1983	Ex Luton & District, 1992
1420	B283KPF	Leyland Tiger TRCTL11/3RH	Plaxton Paramount 3200 IIE	C53F	1985	Ex Luton & District, 1992
1421	SOH553Y	Leyland Tiger TRCTL11/3R	Plaxton Paramount 3200	C50F	1983	Ex Williamsons, Shrewsbury, 1992
1422	CVN174Y	Leyland Tiger TRCTL11/3R	Plaxton Paramount 3200	C53F	1983	Ex Vanguard, Bedworth, 1992
1423	B281KPF	Leyland Tiger TRCTL11/3RH	Plaxton Paramount 3200 IIE	C53F	1985	Ex Luton & District, 1992
1424	LAG314Y	Leyland Tiger TRCTL11/3R	Plaxton Paramount 3200 E	C50F	1983	Ex Parkinson, Welwyn, 1992
1425	B280KPF	Leyland Tiger TRCTL11/3RH	Plaxton Paramount 3200 IIE	C53F	1985	Ex Luton & District, 1992
1426	A909LWU	Leyland Tiger TRCTL11/3R	Plaxton Paramount 3200 E	DP61F	1983	Ex Scutt, Owston Ferry, 1993
1500	B500MPY	Leyland-DAB Tiger Cub	Eastern Coach Works	B46F	1985	
1501	J661UHN	MAN 11.190 HOCL	Optare Vecta	B42F	1992	
1502	J620UHN	MAN 11.190 HOCL	Optare Vecta	B42F	1992	

1503-1543

1503-1543		MAN 11.190 HOCL	Optare Vecta	B42F	1993	*1509-13 are DP42F

1503	K503BHN	1512	K512BHN	1520	L520FHN	1528	L528FHN	1536	L536FHN
1504	K504BHN	1513	K513BHN	1521	L521FHN	1529	L529FHN	1537	L537FHN
1505	K505BHN	1514	K514BHN	1522	L522FHN	1530	L530FHN	1538	L538FHN
1506	K506BHN	1515	K515BHN	1523	L523FHN	1531	L531*FHN	1539	L539FHN
1507	K507BHN	1516	K516BHN	1524	L524FHN	1532	L532FHN	1540	L540FHN
1508	K508BHN	1517	K517BHN	1525	L525FHN	1533	L533FHN	1541	L541FHN
1509	K509BHN	1518	K518BHN	1526	L526FHN	1534	L534FHN	1542	L542FHN
1510	K510BHN	1519	L519FHN	1527	L527FHN	1535	L535FHN	1543	L543FHN
1511	K511BHN								

1590	GLJ486N	Bristol LH6L	Eastern Coach Works	B43F	1975	Ex Trimdon, 1990
1591	GLJ491N	Bristol LH6L	Eastern Coach Works	B43F	1975	Ex Trimdon, 1990

The Westcourt group have 41 MAN 11.190s, all with Optare Vecta bodywork, on order for delivery during 1993. The first of these deliveries were to Tees followed by United and 1515 (K515BHN), of the latter is seen during June 1993 at Spennymoor soon after delivery. The Vecta, like its stablemates the Delta and Spectra, employs Alusuisse construction and shares many common components with them.
John Carter

1592-1618   Bristol LH6L   Eastern Coach Works   B43F   1974   1614 rebodied 1979

| 1592 | WHN592M | 1606 | AHN606M | 1610 | AHN610M | 1614 | GUP898N | 1617 | GUP901N |
| 1600 | WHN600M | 1607 | AHN607M | 1613 | GUP897N | 1616 | GUP900N | 1618 | GUP902N |

| 1619 | HPR395N | Bristol LH6L | | Eastern Coach Works | | B43F | | 1975 | Ex Trimdon, 1990 |

1621-1644   Bristol LH6L   Eastern Coach Works   B43F*   1975   1630 rebodied 1979
*1634 is DP39F

1621	GUP905N	1626	GUP910N	1633	GUP917N	1637	HUP793N	1643	HUP799N
1623	GUP907N	1630	GUP914N	1634	GUP918N	1638	HUP794N	1644	HUP800N
1624	GUP908N	1631	GUP915N	1635	HUP791N	1642	HUP798N		

1646-1699   Bristol LH6L   Eastern Coach Works   B43F   1976-78

1646	LGR646P	1663	NBR663P	1673	NGR673P	1682	NGR682P	1692	XUP692R
1648	LGR648P	1665	NBR665P	1674	NGR674P	1684	NGR684P	1694	CGR894S
1649	LGR649P	1666	NGR666P	1676	NGR676P	1686	STO390R	1695	CGR895S
1650	LGR650P	1667	NGR667P	1677	NGR677P	1687	XPT687R	1696	CGR896S
1651	LGR651P	1668	NGR668P	1678	NGR678P	1688	XPT688R	1697	CGR897S
1658	MGR658P	1669	NGR669P	1679	NGR679P	1689	XPT689R	1698	CGR898S
1660	MGR660P	1670	NGR670P	1680	NGR680P	1691	XUP691R	1699	CGR899S
1661	MGR661P	1672	NGR672P						

1702-1718   Bristol LH6L   Eastern Coach Works   B43F   1978-80   1712/4 ex Provincial, 1984

1702	LPT702T	1706	LPT706T	1711	LPT711T	1714	AFB589V	1717	SUP717V
1703	LPT703T	1709	LPT709T	1712	WAE192T	1715	SUP715V	1718	SUP718V
1704	LPT704T	1710	LPT710T	1713	MUP713T	1716	SUP716V		

1719	YAE515V	Bristol LH6L	Eastern Coach Works	B43F	1980	Ex Rider York, 1991
1900	TPJ56S	Bristol LHS6L	Eastern Coach Works	B34F	1977	Ex Trimdon, 1990
1901	GTX761W	Bristol LHS6L	Eastern Coach Works	DP27F	1980	Ex Trimdon, 1990

1923-1930   Bristol LH6L   Eastern Coach Works   B43F*   1976-80   Ex Trimdon, 1990
*1928 is B45F

| 1923 | JHW123P | 1925 | KHU317P | 1927 | KHU325P | 1928 | KPA347P | 1930 | LMA607P |
| 1924 | KHU316P | 1926 | KHU324P | | | | | | |

1931-1973   Bristol LH6L   Eastern Coach Works   B43F*   1975-80   Ex Trimdon, 1990
*1938/60 are B45F

1931	OCA624P	1940	STT408R	1949	VDV124S	1958	REU324S	1966	WAE294T
1932	OCA627P	1941	STT409R	1950	VDV126S	1959	REU330S	1967	WAE295T
1933	OCA628P	1942	STT410R	1951	VDV128S	1960	SWS769S	1968	YAE512V
1934	OCA629P	1943	STT412R	1952	REU314S	1961	DTL543T	1969	YAE516V
1935	OCA636P	1944	VDV102S	1953	REU316S	1962	DTL546T	1970	YAE517V
1936	OCA638P	1945	VDV103S	1954	REU317S	1963	WAE189T	1971	YAE518V
1937	OCA640P	1946	VDV104S	1955	REU318S	1964	WAE191T	1972	YAE519V
1938	LJT939P	1947	VDV105S	1956	REU322S	1965	WAE193T	1973	AFB586V
1939	TCL137R	1948	VDV106S	1957	REU323S				

2340-2344   Mercedes-Benz L608D   Reeve Burgess   DP19F   1986

| 2340 | C340WHN | 2341 | C341VVN | 2342 | C342VVN | 2343 | C343VVN | 2344 | C344VVN |

2401-2460   Mercedes-Benz L608D   Reeve Burgess   B20F   1986

2401	C401VVN	2423	C423VVN	2431	C431VVN	2445	D645CVN	2453	D653CVN
2402	C402VVN	2424	C424VVN	2432	C432VVN	2446	D646CVN	2454	D654CVN
2403	C403VVN	2425	C425VVN	2433	C433VVN	2447	D647CVN	2455	D655CVN
2404	C404VVN	2426	C426VVN	2434	C434VVN	2448	D648CVN	2456	D656CVN
2405	C405VVN	2427	C427VVN	2441	D641CVN	2449	D649CVN	2457	D657CVN
2420	C420VVN	2428	C428VVN	2442	D642CVN	2450	D650CVN	2458	D658CVN
2421	C421VVN	2429	C429CVN	2443	D643CVN	2451	D651CVN	2459	D659CVN
2422	C422VVN	2430	C430VVN	2444	D644CVN	2452	D652CVN	2460	D660CVN

2464-2480 — Mercedes-Benz L608D — Reeve Burgess — B20F — 1987

2464	D464EAJ	2467	D467EAJ	2470	D470EAJ	2474	D474EAJ	2479	D479EAJ
2465	D465EAJ	2468	D468EAJ	2471	D471EAJ	2477	D477EAJ	2480	D480EAJ
2466	D466EAJ	2469	D469EAJ	2473	D473EAJ	2478	D478EAJ		

2500-2596 — Renault-Dodge S56 — Alexander AM — B25F — 1987

2500	E500HHN	2516	E516HHN	2521	E521HHN	2566	E66KAJ	2581	E581JVN
2501	E501HHN	2517	E517HHN	2522	E522HHN	2568	E68KAJ	2593	E493HHN
2511	E511HHN	2518	E518HHN	2524	E524HHN	2571	E71KAJ	2595	E495HHN
2513	E513HHN	2519	E519HHN	2525	E525HHN	2573	E73KAJ	2596	E496HHN
2515	E515HHN	2520	E520HHN						

3100-3109 — Leyland National 11351A/1R (DAF) — B49F* — 1979 — *3109 is DP49F

3100	LUP900T	3104	LUP904T	3107	RUP307V	3106	PUP506T	3109	RUP309V
3101	LUP901T								

3111-3126 — Leyland National NL116L11/1R — B49F — 1980

3111	UBR111V	3115	APT115W	3118	APT118W	3121	APT121W	3123	APT123W
3112	UBR112V	3116	APT116W	3119	APT119W	3122	APT122W	3126	APT126W
3114	UBR114V	3117	APT117W						

3130-3142 — Leyland National 2 NL116HLXCT/1R — B49F — 1983-84

3130	A130FDC	3134	A134FDC	3136	A136FDC	3138	A138FDC	3142	A142FDC
3131	A131FDC	3135	A135FDC	3137	A137FDC	3140	A140FDC		

The only secondhand Leyland National 2s allocated to United and Tees that did not originate with former NBC fleets are four examples from Blackpool Transport. United 3153 (A543PCW) is seen on service 2 to Bishop Auckland. *Bill Potter*

United's 1233 (C76UHN) is a Leyland Tiger with Duple Dominant bus bodywork and was latterly with the Trimdon Motor Services fleet. It is in Bishops Auckland, returning to the town after performing a school journey. *Keith Grimes*

The arrival of Optare Vectas has reduced the once extensive number of Bristol LHs in the United and Tees fleets. One of the newer examples, 1716 (SUP716V), operating service 762 to Middlesbrough wears the original version of the Tees livery. *Steve Warburton*

The first five of the 1993 delivery of Optare Deltas are allocated to the TMS fleet. The first of these, 4008 (K408BHN), was photographed leaving Middlesbrough bus station on service 11 to Southwood. *Steve Warburton*

The initial batch of Leyland Lynx was allocated to the United depot in Durham, although they have now moved to Bishops Auckland. These vehicles were originally evaluated against the Optare Delta, a process made redundant by the subsequent withdrawal from production of the Lynx. United 5003 (G510EAJ) is seen in Hartlepool working a service that has has its origins in one operated by Gillett Brothers. *Bill Potter*

Thirteen Leyland Lynx 2s are operated by Tees and United. Allocated to Bishop Auckland depot, United's 5012 (J652UHN) is seen entering the bus station in its home town. *G R Mills*

Leaving Darlington bound for Middlesborough is Tees' 3714 a Leyland National, one of the 1977 delivery of over fifty similar vehicles delivered to United. *Bill Potter*

3143	RHG882X	Leyland National 2 NL116AL11/1R (6HLXCT)			B52F	1982	Ex Shearings, 1991
3144	RHG883X	Leyland National 2 NL116AL11/1R			B52F	1982	Ex Shearings, 1991
3145	RHG885X	Leyland National 2 NL116AL11/1R			B52F	1982	Ex Shearings, 1991
3146	RHG887X	Leyland National 2 NL116AL11/1R			B52F	1982	Ex Shearings, 1991
3147	ARN895Y	Leyland National 2 NL116AHLXB/1R			B52F	1982	Ex Shearings, 1991
3148	ARN896Y	Leyland National 2 NL116AHLXB/1R			B52F	1982	Ex Shearings, 1991
3149	ARN897Y	Leyland National 2 NL116AHLXB/1R			B52F	1983	Ex Shearings, 1991
3150	ARN898Y	Leyland National 2 NL116AHLXB/1R			B52F	1983	Ex Shearings, 1991
3151	A541PCW	Leyland National 2 NL116AHLXCT/1R			B49F	1984	Ex Blackpool, 1991
3152	A542PCW	Leyland National 2 NL116AHLXCT/1R			B49F	1984	Ex Blackpool, 1991
3153	A543PCW	Leyland National 2 NL116AHLXCT/1R			B49F	1984	Ex Blackpool, 1991
3154	A544PCW	Leyland National 2 NL116AHLXCT/1R			B49F	1984	Ex Blackpool, 1991
3514	PWY582W	Leyland National 2 NL106L11/1R			B44F	1980	Ex York City & District, 1990

3713-3728

Leyland National 11351A/1R — B49F — 1977

3713	WPT713R	3715	WPT715R	3720	WPT720R	3724	WPT724R	3728	XGR728R
3714	WPT714R	3718	WPT718R	3723	WPT723R	3727	XGR727R		

3730-3739

Leyland National 2 NL116L11/1R — B49F — 1981

3730	MHN128W	3732	MHN130W	3737	RDC737X	3738	RDC738X	3739	RDC739X
3731	MHN129W	3734	RDC734X						

3740	NAT198V	Leyland National 2 NL116L11/1R			B52F	1980	Ex East Yorkshire, 1990
3741	NAT199V	Leyland National 2 NL116L11/1R			B52F	1980	Ex East Yorkshire, 1990
3743	MNW131V	Leyland National 2 NL116L11/1R			B52F	1980	Ex Harrogate & District, 1990
3744	WAO399Y	Leyland National 2 NL116HLXB/1R			B52F	1983	Ex Shearings, 1991
3745	WAO395Y	Leyland National 2 NL116HLXB/1R			B52F	1983	Ex Shearings, 1991
3747	WRA224Y	Leyland National 2 NL116AHLXB/1R			B52F	1983	Ex Trent, 1991
3748	WRA225Y	Leyland National 2 NL116AHLXB/1R			B52F	1983	Ex Trent, 1991
3749	RRA219X	Leyland National 2 NL116AHLXB/1R			B52F	1981	Ex Trent, 1991

4001-4005

DAF SB220LC550 — Optare Delta — B51F — 1990

4001	G209HCP	4002	G210HCP	4003	G211HCP	4004	G212HCP	4005	G214HCP

4006	J866UPY	DAF SB200LC550	Optare Delta	B49F	1992
4007	J867UPY	DAF SB200LC550	Optare Delta	B49F	1992

4008-4022

DAF SB220LC550 — Optare Delta — B49F — 1993

4008	K408BHN	4011	K411BHN	4014	K414BHN	4017	K417BHN	4020	L420FHN
4009	K409BHN	4012	K412BHN	4015	K415BHN	4018	L418FHN	4021	L421FHN
4010	K410BHN	4013	K413BHN	4016	K416BHN	4019	L419FHN	4022	L422FHN

5001-5005

Leyland Lynx LX2R11C15Z4S — Leyland Lynx — B51F — 1990

5001	G508EAJ	5002	G509EAJ	5003	G510EAJ	5004	G511EAJ	5005	G512EAJ

5006-5018

Leyland Lynx LX2R11C15Z4S — Leyland Lynx 2 — B49F — 1991

5006	H31PAJ	5009	H253PAJ	5012	J652UHN	5015	J655UHN	5017	J657UHN
5007	H32PAJ	5010	H254PAJ	5013	J653UHN	5016	J656UHN	5018	J658UHN
5008	H34PAJ	5011	J651UHN	5014	J654UHN				

Livery: Red and cream (United); Red and yellow (Tees); Blue and white (TMS).

Previous Registrations:

A98OVF	A899KAH, ?	LAG314Y	GRH3Y
A949KAJ	A672OKX, 7694VC	LHO992Y	AEF992Y, TBC658
CVN174Y	CDG214Y, 7694VC		

WEARDALE

Weardale Motor Services Ltd, Shittlehopeburn Garage, Stanhope, Co Durham, DL13 3YQ

ADC99A	Leyland Titan PD3/1	Alexander	H42/31F	1959	
BED732C	Leyland Titan PD2/40Sp	East Lancashire	H34/30F	1965	Ex Stanhope, 1993
GUP6H	Leyland Atlantean PDR2/1	Roe	H45/32F	1970	
NPT6J	Leyland Leopard PSU5/4R	Plaxton Elite II	C57F	1971	
TPT6K	Leyland Leopard PSU5/4R	Plaxton Elite II Express	DP68F	1972	
BUP736L	Leyland Leopard PSU5/4R	Plaxton Elite III	C57F	1973	
AUP652L	Bedford VAS5	Plaxton Panorama IV	DP29F	1973	Ex Stanhope, 1993
UPT6N	Leyland Leopard PSU3B/3R	East Lancs EL2000 (1993)	B53F	1974	
GGR307N	Volvo B58-61	Plaxton Elite III	DP68F	1974	
KBR252N	Volvo B58-61	Plaxton Elite III	DP68F	1975	Ex Stanhope, 1993
OJD71R	Bristol LH6L	Eastern Coach Works	B39F	1976	Ex London Transport, 1983
OGR625T	Leyland Leopard PSU3E/3R	Plaxton Supreme III	C53F	1978	
UBR656T	Leyland Leopard PSU3E/3R	Plaxton Supreme IV Express	C53F	1979	
UBR666T	Leyland Leopard PSU3E/3R	Plaxton Supreme IV Express	C53F	1979	
YNL220V	Leyland Atlantean AN68A/2R	MCW	H49/37F	1979	Ex Go-Ahead Northern, 1991
PEF6X	Bedford VAS5	Duple Dominant II	C29F	1981	Ex Stanhope, 1993
C256FHJ	Van Hool TD824	Van Hool Astromega	CH57/27F	1985	Ex Southend, 1991
C666FMP	Volvo B10M-61	Plaxton Paramount 3200 II	C53F	1986	
E965MVN	Mercedes-Benz 609D	Reeve Burgess Beaver	B24F	1988	
F565JBB	CVE Omni	City Vehicle Engineering	B19FL	1988	
F997WPY	Mercedes-Benz 814D	Reeve Burgess Beaver	C33F	1989	
G843BDC	Volvo B10M-60	Plaxton Paramount 3500 III	C51FT	1989	

Livery: red, maroon and cream

Previous Registrations:
ADC99A   6BUP

Arriving in Bishop Auckland is Weardale's Leyland Leopard TPT6K showing the express-door arrangement for the Plaxton Elite II body produced in the early 1970s to meet Bus Grant requirements. It is one of many vehicles in the Weardale fleet over the years to carry the number six.
John Carter

Photographed at the Bishop Auckland end of the Stanhope service, Bristol LH OJD71R is another example from the 95 supplied to London Transport (including three to the London Borough of Hillingdon). There 7'6" width have made them useful vehicles on the second-hand market, many finding their way to the north east, although over twenty remain in the capital. *Keith Grimes*

Weardale operate a pair of Volvo B58s with Plaxton Elite III bodywork. KBR252N, seen here in Newcastle, is one of several coaches in the fleet to have had bus seats fitted, in this case in three and two fashion to accomodate more seats than some older double deckers. *Phillip Stephenson*

WELCOME

Welcome Passenger Services Ltd, 27 Saltmeadows Road, Gateshead, Tyne & Wear, NE8 3AH

Welcome is an autonomous subsidiary of Busways

H401DMJ	Renault S75	Reeve Burgess	B29F	1990	Ex Renault demonstrator 1992
J371BNW	Optare Metrorider	Optare	B29F	1991	
J372BNW	Optare Metrorider	Optare	B29F	1991	
J373BNW	Optare Metrorider	Optare	B29F	1991	
J374BNW	Optare Metrorider	Optare	B29F	1991	
J375BNW	Optare Metrorider	Optare	B29F	1991	
J376BNW	Optare Metrorider	Optare	B29F	1991	
J377BNW	Optare Metrorider	Optare	B29F	1991	
J378BNW	Optare Metrorider	Optare	B29F	1991	
J379BNW	Optare Metrorider	Optare	B29F	1991	
J380BNW	Optare Metrorider	Optare	B29F	1991	
J553NGS	Renault S75	Plaxton Beaver	B28F	1991	
J225JJR	Renault S75	Plaxton Beaver	B28F	1991	
J226JJR	Renault S75	Plaxton Beaver	B28F	1991	
J227JJR	Renault S75	Plaxton Beaver	B28F	1991	
J228JJR	Renault S75	Plaxton Beaver	B28F	1991	
J229JJR	Renault S75	Plaxton Beaver	B28F	1991	
J230JJR	Renault S75	Plaxton Beaver	B28F	1991	
J231JJR	Renault S75	Plaxton Beaver	B28F	1991	
J232JJR	Renault S75	Plaxton Beaver	B28F	1991	
J233JJR	Renault S75	Plaxton Beaver	B28F	1991	
K341PJR	Renault S75	Plaxton Beaver	B28F	1992	
K342PJR	Renault S75	Plaxton Beaver	B28F	1992	
K343PJR	Renault S75	Plaxton Beaver	B28F	1992	
K344PJR	Renault S75	Plaxton Beaver	B28F	1992	
K345PJR	Renault S75	Plaxton Beaver	B28F	1992	
K162FYG	Optare Metrorider	Optare	B29F	1992	
K163FYG	Optare Metrorider	Optare	B29F	1992	
K164FYG	Optare Metrorider	Optare	B29F	1992	
K165FYG	Optare Metrorider	Optare	B29F	1992	
K166FYG	Optare Metrorider	Optare	B29F	1992	
K330RCN	Iveco 59.12	Dormobile Routemaker	B27F	1992	
K331RCN	Iveco 59.12	Dormobile Routemaker	B27F	1992	
K332RCN	Iveco 59.12	Dormobile Routemaker	B27F	1992	
K334RCN	Iveco 59.12	Dormobile Routemaker	B27F	1992	
K335RCN	Iveco 59.12	Dormobile Routemaker	B27F	1992	
K336RCN	Iveco 59.12	Dormobile Routemaker	B27F	1992	
K337RCN	Iveco 59.12	Dormobile Routemaker	B27F	1992	

Livery: Red and yellow

Welcome Passenger Services Ltd have built up a fleet of over 30 midibuses operating frequent bus services on a number of routes in the Newcastle area. The newest vehicles are seven Iveco / Dormobile midibuses such as K334RCN seen here in Grainger Street, Newcastle. *Bill Potter*

All of the Optare Metroriders in the Welcome fleet have been registered in Leeds by the manufacturer, an almost unheard of practice years ago. J373BNW of the 1991 batch was photographed in Grainger Street, Newcastle. *Bill Potter*

YOUR BUS

South Durham Bus Co Ltd, Faverdale Industrial Estate, Darlington, Co Durham,

C325OFL	Ford Transit 190	Dormobile	B16F	1986	Ex Viscount, 1993
C327OFL	Ford Transit 190	Dormobile	B16F	1986	Ex Viscount, 1993
D115DRV	Iveco Daily 49.10	Robin Hood City Nippy	B21F	1986	Ex Harrogate & District, 1993
D472WPM	Iveco Daily 49.10	Robin Hood City Nippy	B21F	1986	Ex Stagecoach South, 1993
D474WPM	Iveco Daily 49.10	Robin Hood City Nippy	B21F	1986	Ex Stagecoach South, 1993
D31KAX	Iveco Daily 49.10	Robin Hood City Nippy	B21F	1986	Ex Hamilton, Maybole, 1993
D44KAX	Iveco Daily 49.10	Robin Hood City Nippy	B21F	1986	Ex Rhondda, 1993
D46KAX	Iveco Daily 49.10	Robin Hood City Nippy	B21F	1986	Ex Rhondda, 1993
D37DNH	Iveco Daily 49.10	Robin Hood City Nippy	B19F	1987	Ex Sherratt, Cold Meece, 1993
D38DNH	Iveco Daily 49.10	Robin Hood City Nippy	B21F	1987	Ex United Counties, 1993
D40DNH	Iveco Daily 49.10	Robin Hood City Nippy	B19F	1987	Ex Sherratt, Cold Meece, 1993
D41DNH	Iveco Daily 49.10	Robin Hood City Nippy	B19F	1987	Ex United Counties, 1993
D547MJA	Iveco Daily 49.10	Robin Hood City Nippy	B21F	1987	Ex Hamilton, Maybole, 1993

Livery: Blue, white and yellow

South Durham, trading as Your Bus, was set up in May 1993 by the former United Automobile md with six frequent services in the Darlington area, in competition with United. The majority of the vehicles in the fleet are Iveco Daily minibuses with Robin Hood City Nippy bodies. New to GM Buses, D547MJA was seen in Darlington Market Place at the end of July 1993. *Bill Potter*

ISBN 1 897990 03 0
Published by *British Bus Publishing*
The Vyne, 16 St Margarets Drive, Wellington,
Telford, Shropshire, TF1 3PH

Printed by Graphics & Print
Unit A13, Stafford Park 15
Telford, Shropshire, TF3 3BB